SPRING ▪ SUMMER 1994/FILM & THEATER

Asian Art & Culture

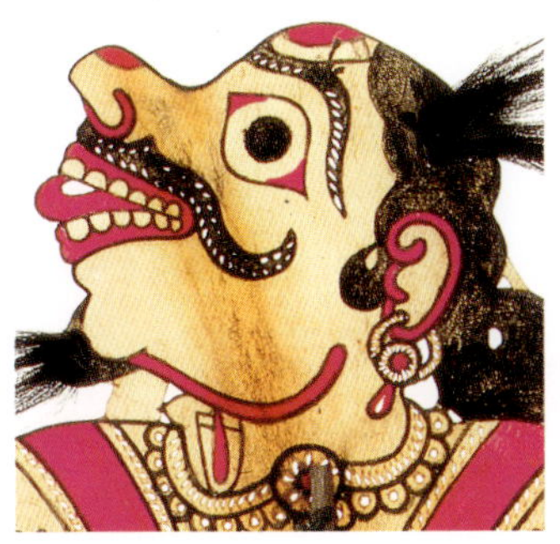
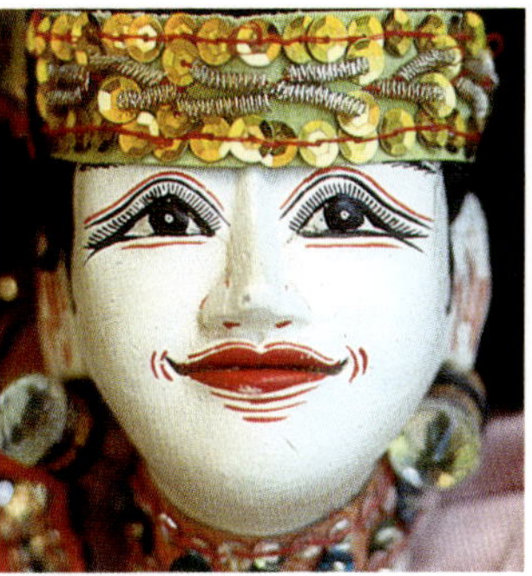
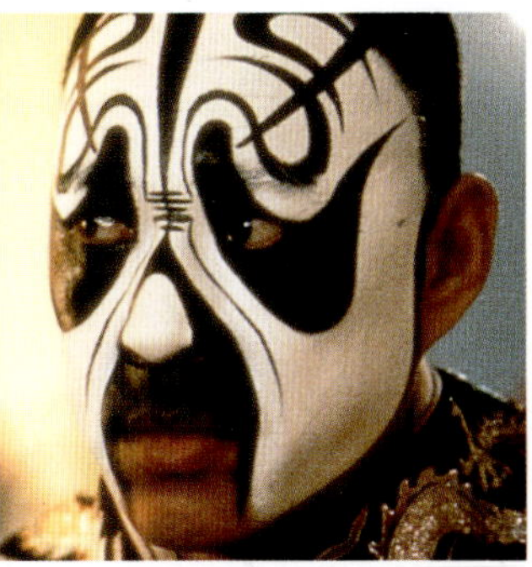

Volume VII, Number 2
Published by
Oxford University Press
in association with the
Arthur M. Sackler Gallery
Smithsonian Institution

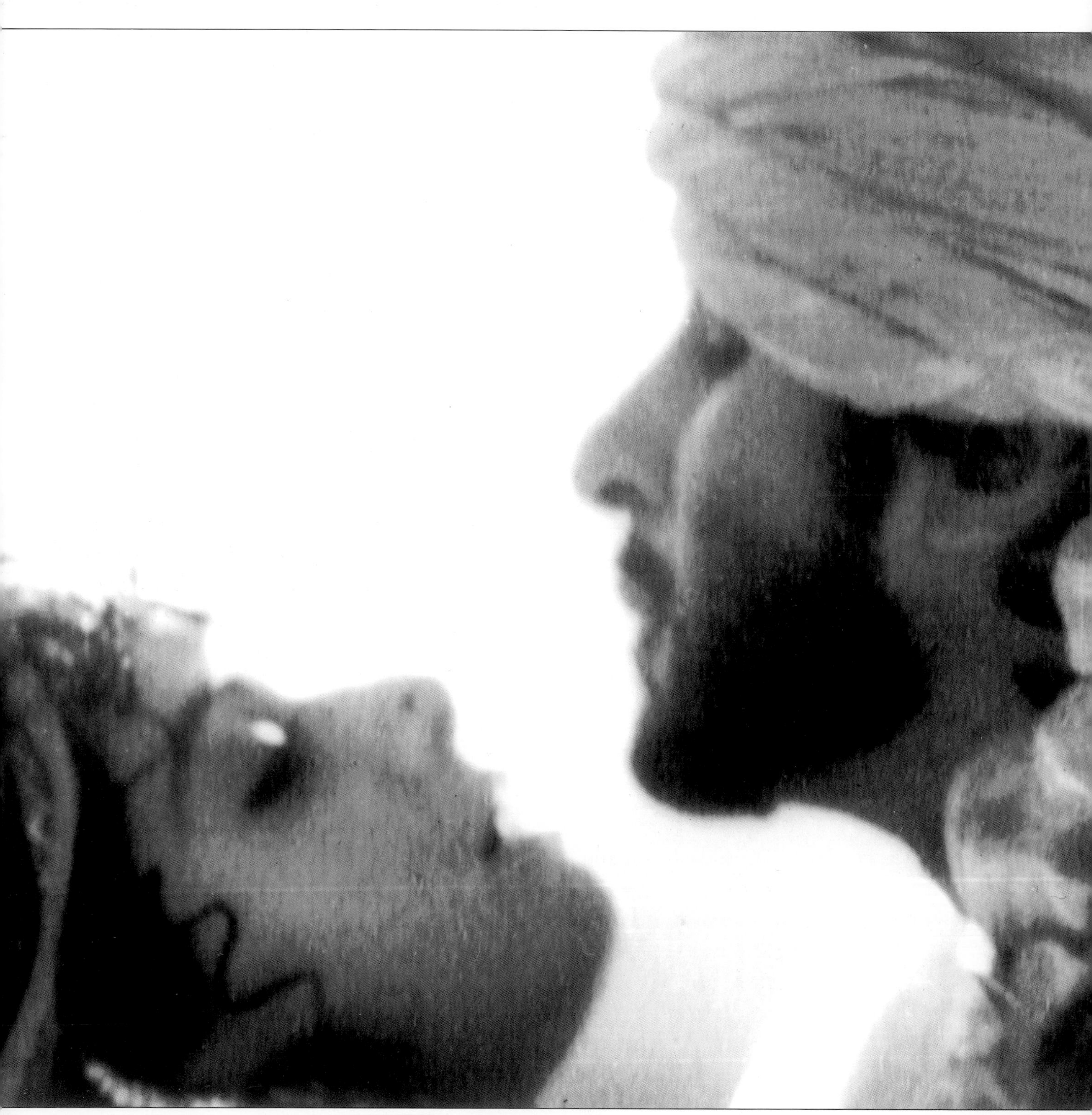

Show Business

The cinema that Raghubir Singh writes about elsewhere in this issue—the work of Satyajit Ray and lesser-known Indian masters like Mrinal Sen, Ritwik Ghatak, G. Aravindan, and Shyam Benegal—is known in India as the "parallel" cinema. "Parallel" is a polite way of saying it is not mainstream. Some of Ray's films have had smaller audiences in India than abroad; his work has won the admiration of the cognoscenti but has little mass appeal. The mainstream Indian cinema is a swirling, muddy flow of cliché and convention, with familiar, even repetitive plots, trite sentiment, stagey stunt scenes, and a profusion of songs and dances. Such films are immensely popular: millions flock to see them in cinema halls around the country, where they often provide the only affordable mass entertainment (and help sustain what is overwhelmingly the world's largest movie industry). Many of these movies are made in Bombay's filmland, a throbbing hub of cinematic enterprise that has been dubbed "Bollywood."

In my novel Show Business *I have attempted to focus on this world through the life and times of an imaginary superstar, Ashok Banjara. In the process I have tried to examine, as I did in my first novel,* The Great Indian Novel, *the kinds of stories Indian society tells about itself—except that, where I had earlier drawn inspiration from myth and the legends of the* Mahabharata, *I looked in this novel at the modern myths purveyed by popular cinema and the tinsel myths surrounding the lives of those who make these movies. My novel pursues this tack in three interlocking narratives—Ashok's recollections of various stages of his career; the stories, complete with tongue-in-cheek lyrics, of the films in which he and other characters from the novel perform at the time; and monologues addressed to him by family and friends as he lies immobilized in a hospital bed. Through them emerges a portrait of the world of Indian cinema in which there is little place for the sensibility and technical sophistication of a Satyajit Ray. While the extracts that follow are fiction, not reportage, they are faithful to the environment they describe.*

This is how the novel begins:

I can't believe I'm doing this.

Me, Ashok Banjara, product of the finest public school in independent India, Secretary of the Shakespeare Society at St. Francis' College, no less, not to mention son of the Minister of State for Minor Textiles, chasing an ageing actress round a papier-maché tree in an artificial drizzle, lip-synching to the tinny inanities of an aspiring (and highly aspirating) playback-singer. But it *is* me, it's my mouth that's moving in soundless ardour, it's my feet that are scudding treeward in faithful obeisance to the unlikely choreography of the dance director. Move, step, turn, as sari-clad Abha, yesterday's heart-throb, old enough to be my mother and just about beginning to show it, nimbly evades my practiced lunge and runs, famous bust

■ Sridevi (left) and Amitabh Bachchan star in *God Is My Witness* (1993), the story of two rival Pathan clans in Afghanistan. Badshah Khan (Bachchan) discovers that his greatest opponent is a woman, the beautiful Benazir, played by Sridevi.

outthrust, to the temporary shelter of an improbably leafy branch. I follow, head tilted back, arms outstretched, pretending to sing:

I shall always chase you
To the ends of the earth,
I want to embrace you
From Pahelgaon to Perth,
My love!

My arms encircle her, but as my fingertips meet, she ducks, dancing, and slips out of my clutches, pirouetting gaily away. Drenched chiffon clings to the pointed cones of her blouse, but she raises one end of the soaked sari *pallav* to half-cover her face, holding the edge across the bridge of her perfect nose in practiced coyness. Her large eyes imprison me, then blink in release. Despite myself, I marvel. She has done this for twenty years: it is my first attempt.

I shall always chase you
From now 'til my rebirth
And it's only when I face you
That I feel I know my worth,
My love!

I shall always chase you,
I'll never feel the dearth
Of my desire to lace you
Around my . . .

"Cut!" I am caught in mid-gesture, mid-movement, mid-word. The playback track screeches to a stop. I freeze, feeling as foolish as I imagine I must look. Abha snaps her irritation, turns away.

"No, no, no!" The dance director is waddling furiously towards me. He is fat and dark, but nothing if not expressive: his hands are trembling, his kohl-lined eyes are trembling, the layers and folds of flesh on his bare torso are trembling. "How many times I am telling you! Like this!" Hands, feet and trunk describe arabesques of motion. "Not this!" He does a passable imitation of a stiff-necked paraplegic having a seizure. The technicians laugh. I smile nervously, looking furtively at my co-star. Abha stands apart from us, hands on hips in a posture of fury. But am I imagining it, or is there something softer around her eyes as she looks at me?

I open hapless hands to the dance director, palms facing him in a gesture of concession. "Okay, okay, Masterji. Sorry."

“Sorry? Is *my* good name you will be ruining. What-all is this, they will be saying. Gopi Master has forgotten what is dance.” His pectorals quiver in indignation. “For you maybe doesn’t matter. You are *bachcha.* I am having fifteen years in this business. What they will say about me, hanh?”

I shrug my embarrassment. I thought I’d done what I had been told to do, but that doesn’t seem the right thing to say. Gopi Master stamps his feet, one oily ringlet of black hair falling over a flashing red eye. He tosses his curls and strides off.

“Okay, okay.” This is the director, Mohanlal. Mohanlal looks like a lower divisional clerk: he wears a fraying white cotton shirt, black trousers, thick glasses and a perpetually harassed expression. Right now it is even more harassed than usual. I am evolving a Mohanlal Scale of High Anxiety, ranging from the pained visage with which he embarks on any second take (1 on the scale) to the extreme angst that furrows his face when the Producer-Sahib visits and wants to know why the film isn’t finished yet (10). My terpsichoric incompetence has him up at about 5, but he is teetering on the edge of 6. I try to look earnest and willing.

“Okay,” says Mohanlal for the third time. “Let’s get back to this. Abhaji, I am sorry. Just once more, please, I promise you. Right, Ashokji? We’ll get it right this time.”

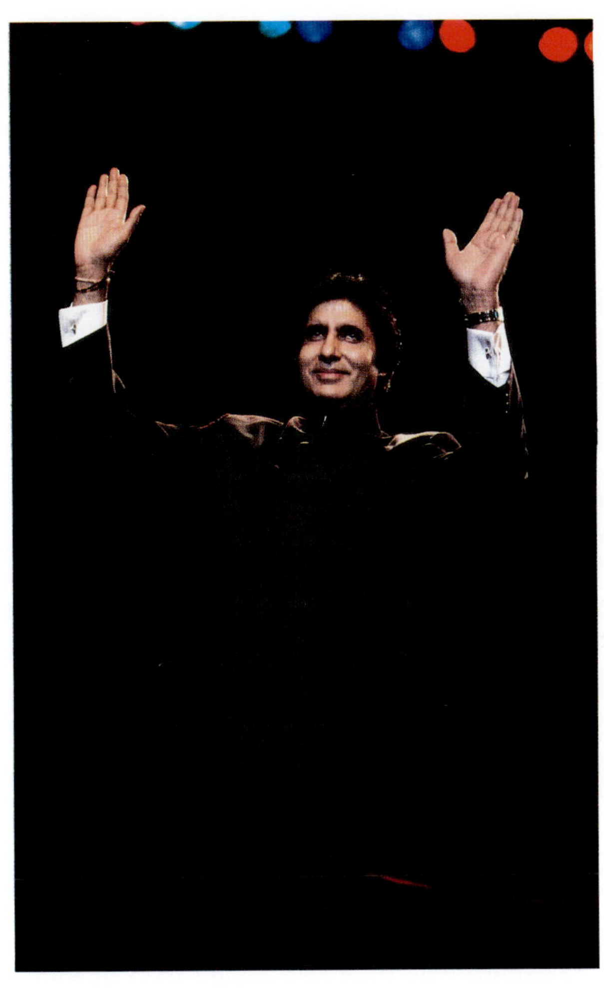

■ Amitabh Bachchan, one of Indian cinema’s superstars, salutes at the Natraj Awards ceremony, New York, 1991

“Right,” I respond, without confidence.

“Okay, clear the stage.” Mohanlal’s instructions emerge in the mildest tone. One of the producer’s sidekicks, standing beyond the arc lights, claps his hands to reinforce them, like a manual relay station. The clapper boy holds his board up for the start of the take. I grin at Abha, hoping for sympathy. She averts her gaze.

“Lights! Camera! Action!”

. . . The playback song starts again, I lip-synch my melodic vow of eternal pursuit, the rain falls through holed buckets, my feet move as they have been taught, but I am terrified they will trip over each other. I am acutely aware of the ridiculousness of what I am doing, even more aware of the incompetence with which I am doing it. Double embarrassment here, to be doing the ridiculous incompetently. I am so petrified with fear of failure that I do not sense the tickle in my nose until I reach for Abha in mid-cavort, my back impossibly bent in choreographical adulation, one hand behind my rump like a bureaucrat seeking a discreet bribe, the other stretching up to her chin, lips moving to the playback lyric. I am hardly aware of it as I look into her eyes, my nostrils flaring in desire, and sneeze.

■ Rahul Roy and Pooja Bedi, popular heartthrobs of Indian movies, perform at the Natraj Awards ceremony, New York, 1991.

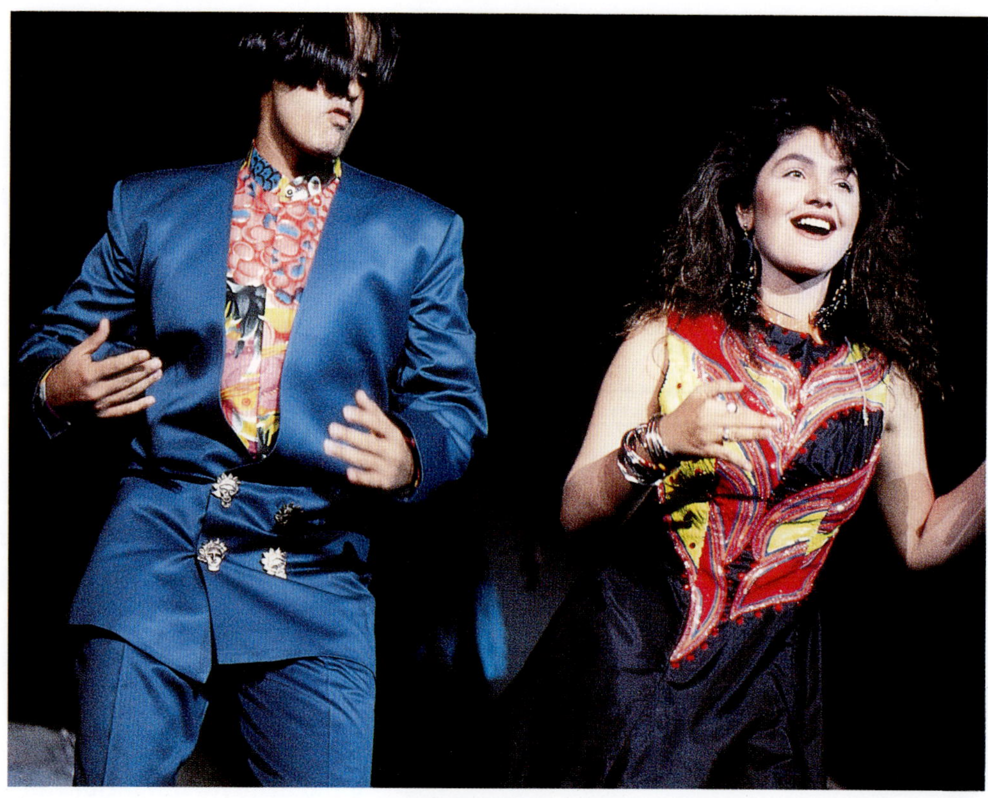

"Cut!"

"Oh Christ," I mutter under my breath, reaching for my handkerchief. I am not Christian, but fourteen years of Catholic education have taught me a fine line in blasphemy.

All hell breaks loose. As I sneeze again, I see Gopi Master, beside himself, launching into a paroxysmal frenzy that could easily be set to music in his next film. I see Abha throwing up her hands and stalking off towards her dressing room. . . . Mohanlal's anxiety is 8 on the scale, and climbing.

"But she can't do this to me!" Mohanlal begins, quite literally, to tear out his hair, his long fingers running outward through the thinning strands like refugees fleeing in despair, taking with them what they can. "We're behind schedule as it is. . . ."

Ashok recovers from his disastrous start, and within a few years becomes a superstar:

Back to work. I am no longer entirely sure where, and to which film. I now have a secretary who schedules me, thrusts a piece of paper into the chauffeur's hand and sends me on my way, sometimes to do three films in the two shooting shifts theoretically available. In most Bombay studios, these are 9:30 a.m. to 5:30 p.m. (the day shift), and 6 p.m. to midnight (the evening, or more realistically night, shift). In my early days I would have been lucky to have enough work to need to shoot every day, but now I am so over-committed I can't meet my obligations within the two shifts possible. "Gimme dates," scream the producers, sounding like socially-starved American teenagers, "gimme dates." So my secretary, the efficient Subramanyam, gives them dates, and sometimes they're the same dates for three different producers. Which means I shuttle back and forth, leaving one shift early and arriving at the next one late, sometimes decamping after one shot and promising to be back for the next, not always keeping the promises. What the hell, the films seem to get made anyway, and as long as they have my name on them they don't do too badly at the box office.

It's not as if I'm being worked to the bone or anything. Any period of film shooting consists of bursts of frenetic activity interspersed with long bouts of hanging around waiting for people to set things up: scenes, lighting, equipment. In one eight hour shift the director will probably expose anything from 1200 to 3000 feet of film, the exact figure depending on how undemanding he is, how competent his crew and cast are, and how many technical things that can go wrong do go wrong. There's about 90 to 95 feet of celluloid to every minute of filmed action, so the *most* productive crew actually gets about half an hour's worth of film into the can at the end of an eight-hour shift—and most don't manage half of that. Of that footage, no more than one-fifth actually survives the cutting-room floor and gets included in the movie itself. Which means that each shift actually contributes something like three to six minutes to the movie people pay to see in the hall.

"Have I shot anything for this film already?" I ask the secretary as I am about to leave. The film's name means nothing to me, but then most Hindi film names mean nothing to anybody.

"Yes, sir," replies my efficient Subramanyam. "You have done two shootings

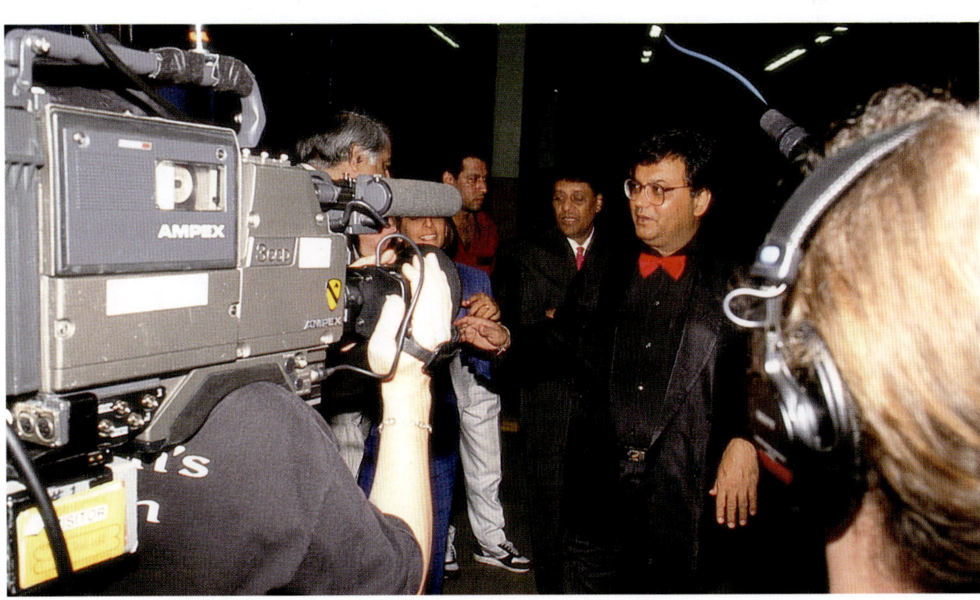

■ Subhash Ghai, center, director of numerous Indian films, has been called India's "Spielberg." Here he attends the Natraj Awards ceremony held in New York, 1991.

already, sir, last month. One-and-half shifts."

"One-and-*a*-half, Subramanyam," I chide him gently. "You don't know what it's about, do you?"

Subramanyam looks bashful. "No, sir, I am not knowing."

"Well, I guess I'll find out," I concede. "There'll be plenty more shifts to catch up with the story."

For a big film I'd have to put in, as the star, anything from twenty to thirty shifts myself. When I'm doing half a dozen films simultaneously, some of them shot in locations far away from the other directors' studios, "gimme dates" becomes a plaintive cry. I used to think that a movie that took three years to make actually involved people toiling every day for three years. Not a bit of it: all that probably happened was that the producer had too ambitious a cast, and he couldn't get dates. It's worst of all when both the hero and the heroine are stars in great demand: the dates he gives may not coincide with hers, and you can't shoot love scenes on different shifts.

■ Advertisements for movies are found throughout many Indian cities. Images such as this one in Bangalore, Karnataka, document the ever-present disparity between the make-believe world of the movies (as represented by the poster) and the reality of daily life at street level.

I turn up at Himalaya Studios and am hustled into costume: synthetic sweatshirt, blue baseball cap, unfashionably unfaded jeans and canvas shoes. A dirty white handkerchief is knotted hastily around my neck. I am some sort of local tough, defender of the neighborhood and general all-purpose good guy, who will of course go on to demolish the villains and marry the rich heroine.

"What's supposed to happen here?" I ask the director, as the make-up man puts

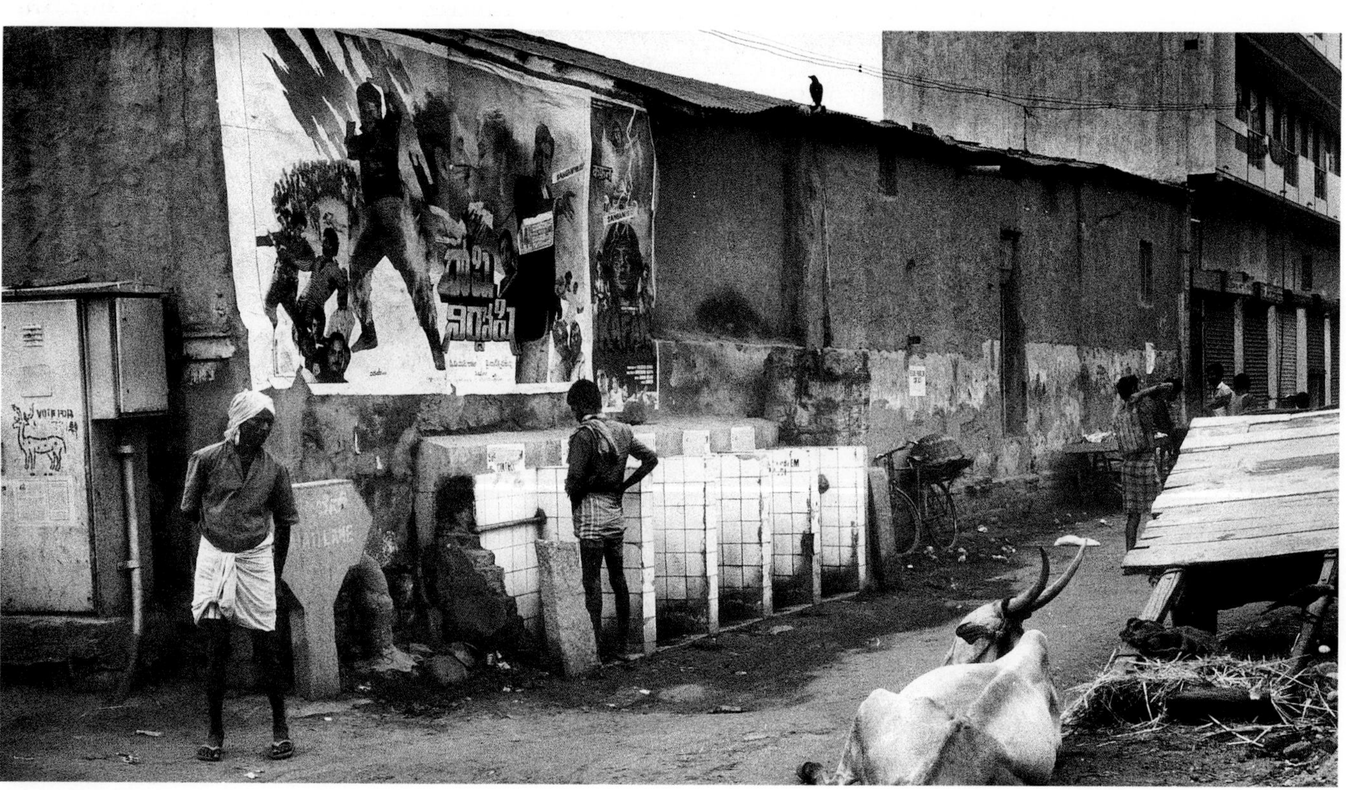

on the necessary traces of blush to heighten the rosiness of my cheeks. Nearly thirty years since Independence, but we still associate pink skin with healthiness.

"We're ready to shoot," he says, trying to sound efficient and in charge. He's a young fellow, some producer's son, known to everybody, even me who's his age, as The Boy.

"Congratulations, but that's not what I meant," I reply. "What are we ready to shoot?" I have long since given up looking at scripts: there are too many of them and they all read alike, and in any case it's too much to keep up with three convoluted plot-lines a day.

"Oh. I see what you mean." The Boy is quick to catch on: it's clear he knows his profession. "It's an outdoor shot. Heroine's car breaks down, some rowdies start bothering her, you go and tell them to buzz off, bash them up when they don't, open the hood and fix the car. Simple."

"Straightforward," I agree. "Any deathless dialogue in this one, or can I make it up as I go along?"

The director looks dubious. "Just the line when you first tell them to buzz off—there's some good stuff in there, I think. Something about haven't they got mothers and sisters. The rest you can ad lib."

"Good." The make-up man is finished. "Lead me to it."

There is only one outdoor locale at Himalaya, which is not small as Bombay studios go. This is a street that runs past the studio's administration office and canteen, into a clump of bushes and flowering trees that could serve, if shot from the right angles, as a low-budget setting for romantic rural interludes. A red Fiat is already parked on the street, and there seems to be a girl in it, though from where I am approaching her, most of her face is obscured by a large straw hat. As I step out onto the street a ragged cheer goes up from the throng of hangers-on who always seem to manage to get in to the studio grounds. I wave grandly back at them, taking care not to walk close enough to be touched or importuned for autographs.

The director comes up with a closely-typed page from the screenplay containing the dialogue he wants me to remember. I dismiss the proffered sheet: "read it to me," I say. The make-up man, a fat dark chap with a front-pocket full of combs and brushes, hovers around, examining me critically in the bright sunlight. The mirror in his hand catches the light and reflects it into my eye as I am listening to The Boy, so I shoo him away with a gesture of irritation. He backs off, and continues to examine me from a safer distance, the mirror turned away from my eyes.

The rowdies, in tight-fitting tee-shirts and corduroy pants, mill about the car, trying to chat up the straw hat. The inevitable Arriflex camera (every Indian cinematographer uses Arriflex, it's as if they've never heard of any other brand) stands on a steel tripod, pointing at them. The electrical equipment is now in place, principally a blue wooden box the size of a car battery (for all I know, it might well have

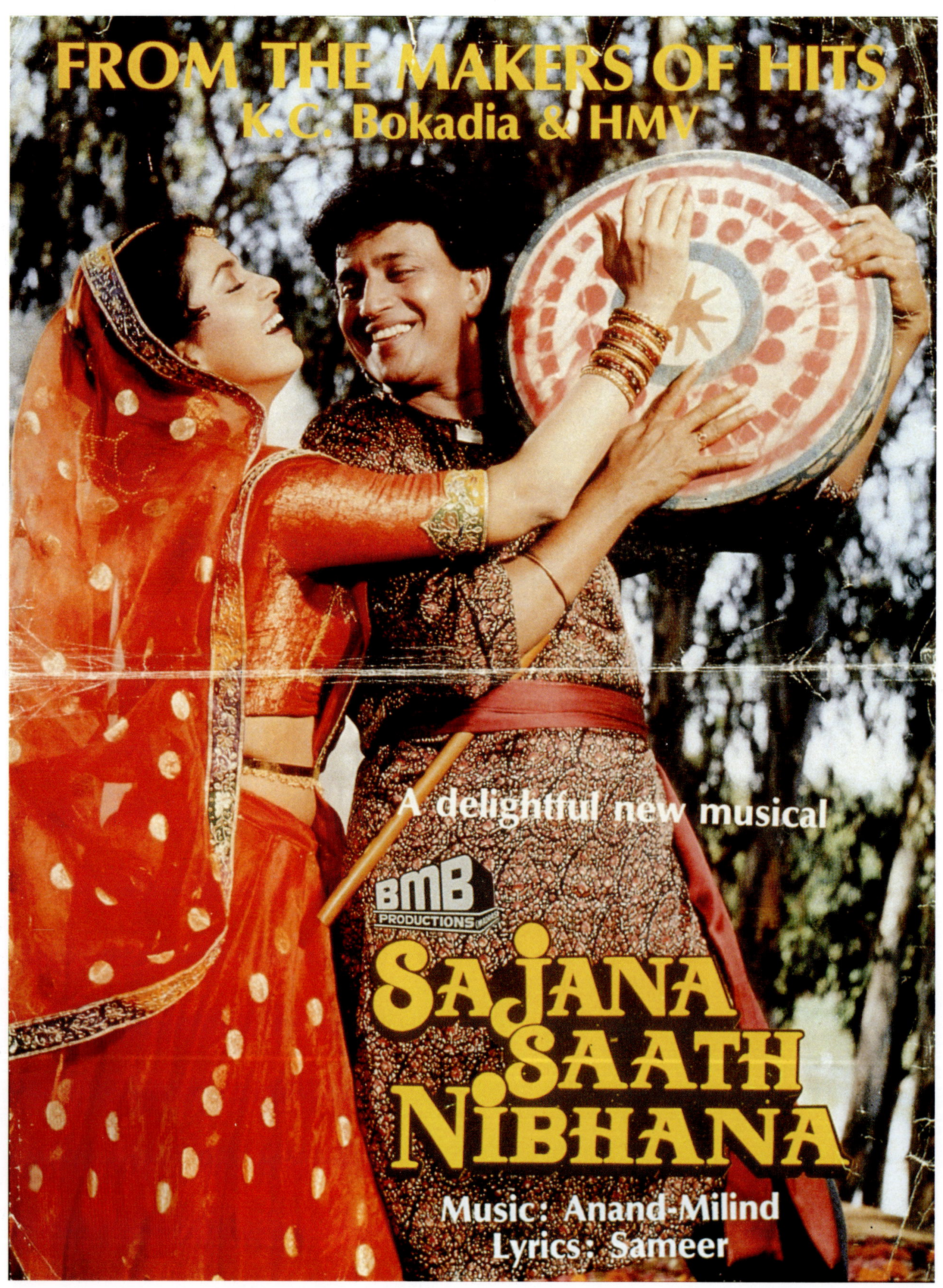
FROM THE MAKERS OF HITS
K.C. Bokadia & HMV
A delightful new musical
BMB
PRODUCTIONS
SAJANA
SAATH
NIBHANA
Music: Anand-Milind
Lyrics: Sameer

■ Indian film poster for the musical *Sajana Saath Nibhan*

been a car battery in an earlier incarnation) capped by three fuse-boxes and sporting an array of sockets on the side, from which sprout a profusion of wires of every color. The technicians, dark dusty men in dirty *chappals* wearing checked shirts that hang out of their trousers, are sitting around on makeshift wooden stools, waiting for me. Let them wait.

They're not the only ones. In one cluster of folding chairs on the other side of the street sit unknown stalwarts of the production team, chatting, reading Hindi newspapers, drinking tea, seemingly disengaged from the day's events. God knows who they are, or what their role is. Every unit I've seen seems to have some fifty people on its payroll at each shift, about twenty of whom are completely idle at any given time.

I've absorbed the mothers and sisters bit in the dialogue. "Got it," I confirm.

"Ready for action?" The Boy asks.

"Sure. But you're not." I point up the steps we've just descended, where a fading board proclaims *Himalaya Studio.* "Aren't you going to do anything about that?" My hand sweeps from the camera to the board.

"Salim!" The director yells. A scruffy boy shuffles past, bearing a sign far too large for him that says "State Bank of India." The last time I'd been here the Himalaya administration building had masqueraded as a hospital. The lad awkwardly drags the sign up the steps. None of the twenty idle people move to help him.

"Who's in the straw hat?" I ask the director conversationally as the sign is being switched.

"Your heroine," The Boy responds, as if astonished by the question.

"I gathered that," I reply cuttingly. "But *who* is my heroine in this picture?"

The director looks mortally offended. "Mehnaz Elahi," he tells me.

"Never heard of her," I admit cheerfully. "Have I met her?"

I am not just being crass. There is a flood of new actresses washing up at the feet of producers these days. With the problems they are having getting dates for the handful of recognized big name females who can still draw crowds at the box-office (as poor Abha, falsies notwithstanding, no longer can) one way out for many producers is to cast an established hero against an "up-and-coming" heroine. I don't mind too much, because this new crop of heroines is good-looking, articulate and largely uninhibited. The periods of enforced idleness at every shooting pass very pleasantly indeed in their company.

"I think she was at the *muhurat,*" the director says, "but I remember you made only a fleeting appearance."

"Ah, yes, that's possible." I am slightly embarrassed. The *muhurat* of any film, the auspicious moment when the opening shot is canned, is not an event its star is supposed to miss. But Subramanyam had, bless him, "given dates."

"Okay, the sign's up," says The Boy. "Let's go." The cameraman takes up

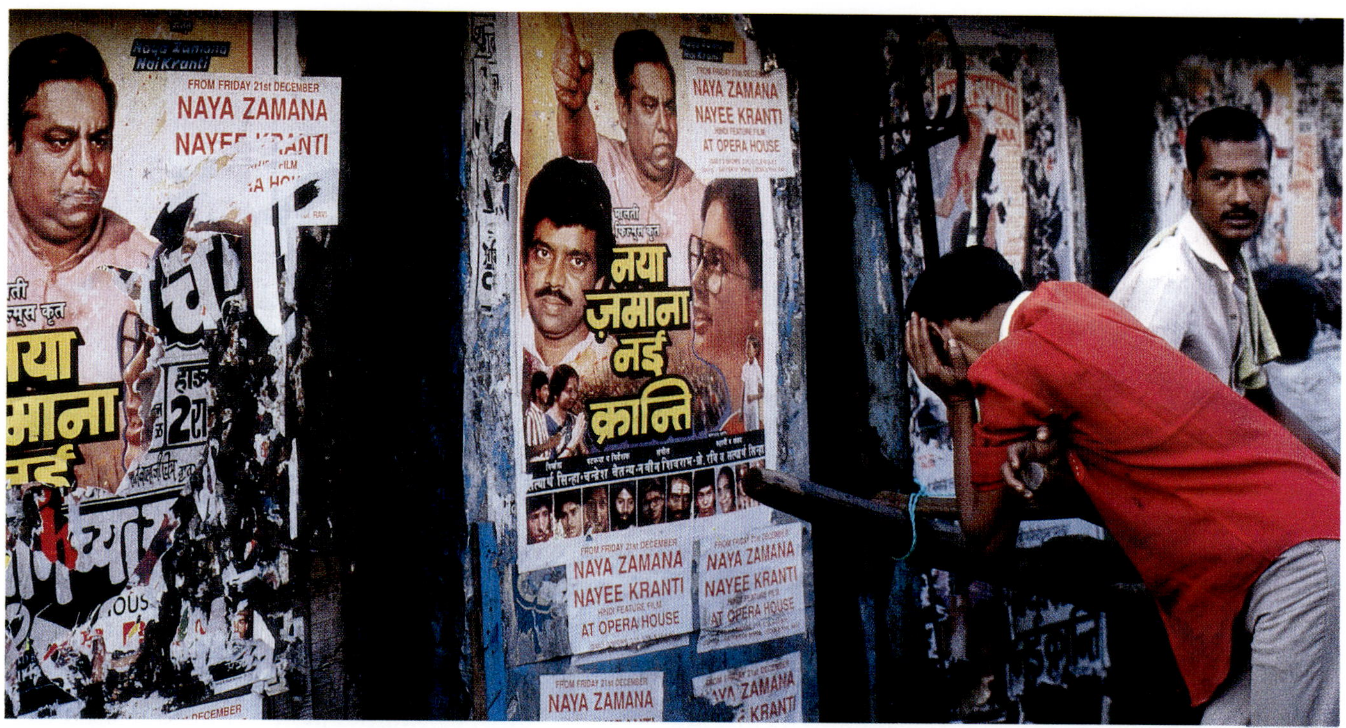

■ Cart pullers wait for work in front of a wall covered with movie posters in Bombay. The ubiquitous presence of movie posters and advertising art in India attests to the industry's popularity and the need for escapist entertainment.

position. So do the rowdies. A sound man crouches behind the car, holding a mike on a fishing rod.

"Start sound! Camera! Action!"

The rowdies begin their harassment. The girl in the straw hat looks helpless. I march in, upbraid them. They are not much impressed by my invocation of their mothers and sisters. They are more impressed by my fists. This is not a choreographed stunt scene, merely an impromptu thrashing. One or two of my blows almost make contact, but I manage to stop just short, knowing from prior carelessness how painful sore hands can be. They turn tail and flee. I turn to the damsel I have rescued from her distress.

"That takes care of them," I begin. And then I dry up completely.

For the car door opens, just as it is supposed to, and out steps the most beautiful woman I have ever seen. She takes off her straw hat, and I am at a complete loss for words.

"Cut!" says the director. He strides into the frame. "What happened?" he demands. "You're supposed to say, can I help . . . ." He stops, because it is apparent I am not listening to him. Nor is the girl. She is looking directly at the expression on my face, and an intuitive smile is playing at the corners of her mouth.

"Oh," says The Boy, taking this in. "Ashok Banjara, meet Mehnaz Elahi."

"Hello," she says. Her voice reaches deep inside me and strums a responsive chord. An echo emerges: "hello," I say.

"Well, now that we've got that out of the way," says the director impatiently, "can we try that shot again? Only this time, you're supposed to say . . . ."

I get through that shift in a trance-like state. At the first opportunity, when Mehnaz has disappeared for a costume change, I ring Subramanyam.

"Change my dates a bit this month," I instruct him. "I want to give priority to this young director's film. Give him whatever shifts he wants."

"I am doing, sir," Subramanyam confirms disapprovingly, "but many producers not being happy with you. I just warning you, sir."

"Good man," I tell him. "Now give The Boy all the dates he wants, okay? And one more thing—find out all you can for me about Mehnaz Elahi."

Ashok goes on, as several Hindi film stars have done in real life, to enter a bigamous relationship with Mehnaz. It is his heroic screen image, though, that propels him into politics through a stunning victory at the polls. But the venture is not a success; Ashok returns to films, has a serious accident on set, and is hospitalized.

Of course, the issues of good and evil, right and wrong, which are so much the staple of Hindi cinema, are less clear to critics of the industry. Later in the novel, Ashok's brother, Ashwin, talks to him at the hospital about the views of the stock villain, Pranay:

Did you know that Pranay's some sort of closet Commie? Oh, very restrained and reflective and all that, but overflowing with conviction and jargon. "I was not surprised when Ashok entered bourgeois politics," he said to me, well out of Dad's hearing, thank God. *Bourgeois* politics—can you imagine? "After all, every Hindi film hero is ontologically a counter-revolutionary." He said that, really, "ontologically." I had to look it up in the dictionary afterwards. And I don't think he's even been to college. Where do these guys pick up this crap from?

"A counter-revolutionary?" I asked, incredulously. "How?" He acquired this terribly intense expression, all beetle-brows and outthrust jaw. "Because they serve, unconsciously or otherwise, to dissipate the revolutionary energies of the masses," he replied. "The frustrations and aspirations that would fuel the masses' struggle for justice is sidetracked by being focused on the screen success of a movie star. The proletariat's natural urge to overthrow injustice is vicariously fulfilled in the hero's defeat of the straw villain—me." I swear the guy didn't even smile. "Films in India are truly the opiate of the people; by providing an outlet to their pent-up urges, the Bombay films make them forget the injustice of the oppressive social order. Evil is personalized in the villain, rather than in the system which makes victims, not heroes, of us all. A false solution is found when the villain is vanquished, and the masses go home happy. The ownership and control of the means of production remain unchanged."

Absurd, of course, but can you believe words like these coming out of the mouth-of a Bollywood type? Especially this fellow, with his white shoes and ridiculous ties? And there was more, believe it or not. To make conversation more than anything else, I found myself saying something about the melting of class and caste barriers in Hindi movies. . . . He objected quite strongly. "It is just the opposite. Romantic love across caste and class lines," he declared solemnly, "is used to cast a veil over the classic contradictions inherent in these situations. It is an exploitative device to blur the reality of class struggle by promoting an illusion of class mobility. Instead of making the revolutionary youth want to overthrow the landlord, the Hindi film promises him he can marry the landlord's daughter. The classless cuddle," he concluded, "is capitalist camouflage."

"You ought to enter politics yourself," I suggested half-jokingly, only to receive an earful about the bourgeois parliamentary system.

Speaking about the proletariat, though, you know we've kept them out of here. I'm afraid a combination of hospital rules and security considerations have left the great unwashed in the courtyard even as we troop in to the Intensive Care Unit for these measured monologues. . . . Anyway, what I wanted to tell you was that on my way in I spoke to one of the fellows waiting outside. He was, would you believe it, a rickshawallah, condemned to a short and brutish life pulling human loads far too heavy for him through rough and pitted streets in rain and heatwave alike. He had spent all his savings to take a train from Calcutta to come and watch anxiously for your recovery. Somebody presented him to me and I stopped and talked, not just because I felt I had to but because I was genuinely curious about what you meant to this man—a man who had, in effect, abandoned his livelihood to be by your bedside, or as close to it as he could get. Why did he like your pictures, I asked him.

He liked the action, he replied in Darbhanga-accented Hindi. Ashokji was a master of action, stunts, fights. He didn't like pictures without action: if there is no action, he asked, what is there to see?

And this action, what did it represent for him?

The triumph of right over wrong, he said. The victory of *dharma.* The reassertion of the moral order of the universe. Ashokji was the upholder of Right: for this reason, he was like an *avatar* of God. The other *avatars,* Rama, Krishna, maybe even Buddha and Gandhi, are all worshipped, but they lived a long time ago and it was difficult to identify really with any of them. Ashok Banjara, though, lived today: his deeds could be seen on the silver screen, for the price of a day's earnings. And it is as if God has come down to earth to make himself visible to ordinary men. For me, Sahib, he said, Ashokji *is* a god.

I left him, strangely humbled by the purity of his devotion to you, and trudged up the stairs into the hospital. I'm afraid I forgot to ask him his name.

As Ashok lies in hospital, he makes the best case he can for his profession, and his life:

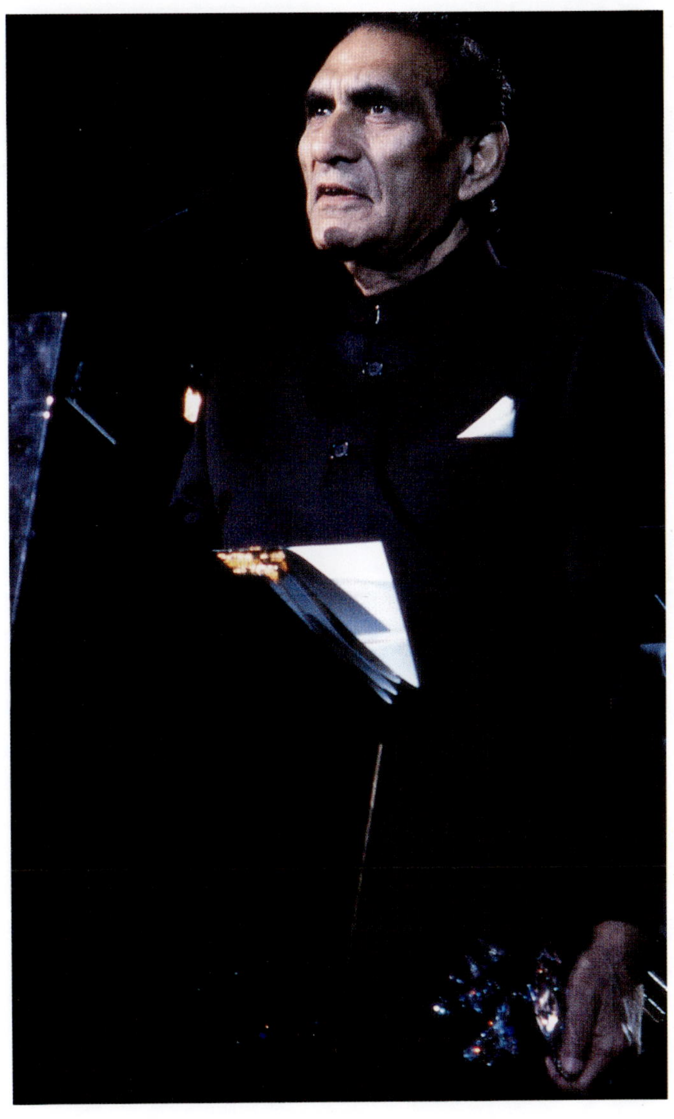

■ B. R. Chopra, director, speaks at the Natraj Awards ceremony, New York, 1991.

I don't know what they can do to give [my life] back to me; I feel it slipping away, like the wet sari of a dancing actress. For the moment I hold it in my hands, I can feel its texture and its wetness, sense the shape of the body to which it is attached, but I also know that with each twist of her hips, each choreographed shake of her bust, she is taking the sari out of my outstretched grasp. And that in the end the rain will still keep coming down, the music will continue playing, but I will be left holding nothing but my own emptiness.

. . . But what about the masses, the great public whom no one would let into this hospital? They came from everywhere and nowhere to see me, from the 6,000 cinemas of our land they walked and trudged and took trains and rode to see me, from huts and hovels and *dhabas* and hotels they travelled to see me, and no one let them in. . . . *They* are my true intimates, I want to shout to the doctors. It is in their lives, their hearts, that my legacy lies. Allow them in, they will numb my pain, they will revive me.

For doctor, there is much I have given them, huddled as they are in a world of little work and low wages, cramped space and closed prospects, social tyranny and perpetual struggle. I embodied their alternative, their other life. To invent something that is beyond reality, to incarnate escape and by so doing to make it true—as true as anything else they have ever known, and infinitely more pleasurable: that is what I have done, and done better than anybody else. I bestrode the cinema screen and I reified the dreams of millions, saying to them: look, in me, Ashok Banjara, you can see your dreams come alive while you are awake, you can take my fate in your hands and we can triumph together. I have kept India awake by telling the nation they can dream with their eyes open. I have given each Indian the chance to reinvent his life, to thrill to the adventurous chase, to chase the unattainable girl, to attain the most glorious victory, to glory in the sheer joy of living. I have brought dignity to innumerable lives, doctor; more, I have brought hope.

The same hope that they are now holding out for me in their vigils outside this hospital. Let them touch me with it, doctor. Allow them to heal me with the truth of their devotion, as I have lifted them with my own truth. Yes, truth: for what I have done is to take a part, a situation, a line of dialogue, an expression, a

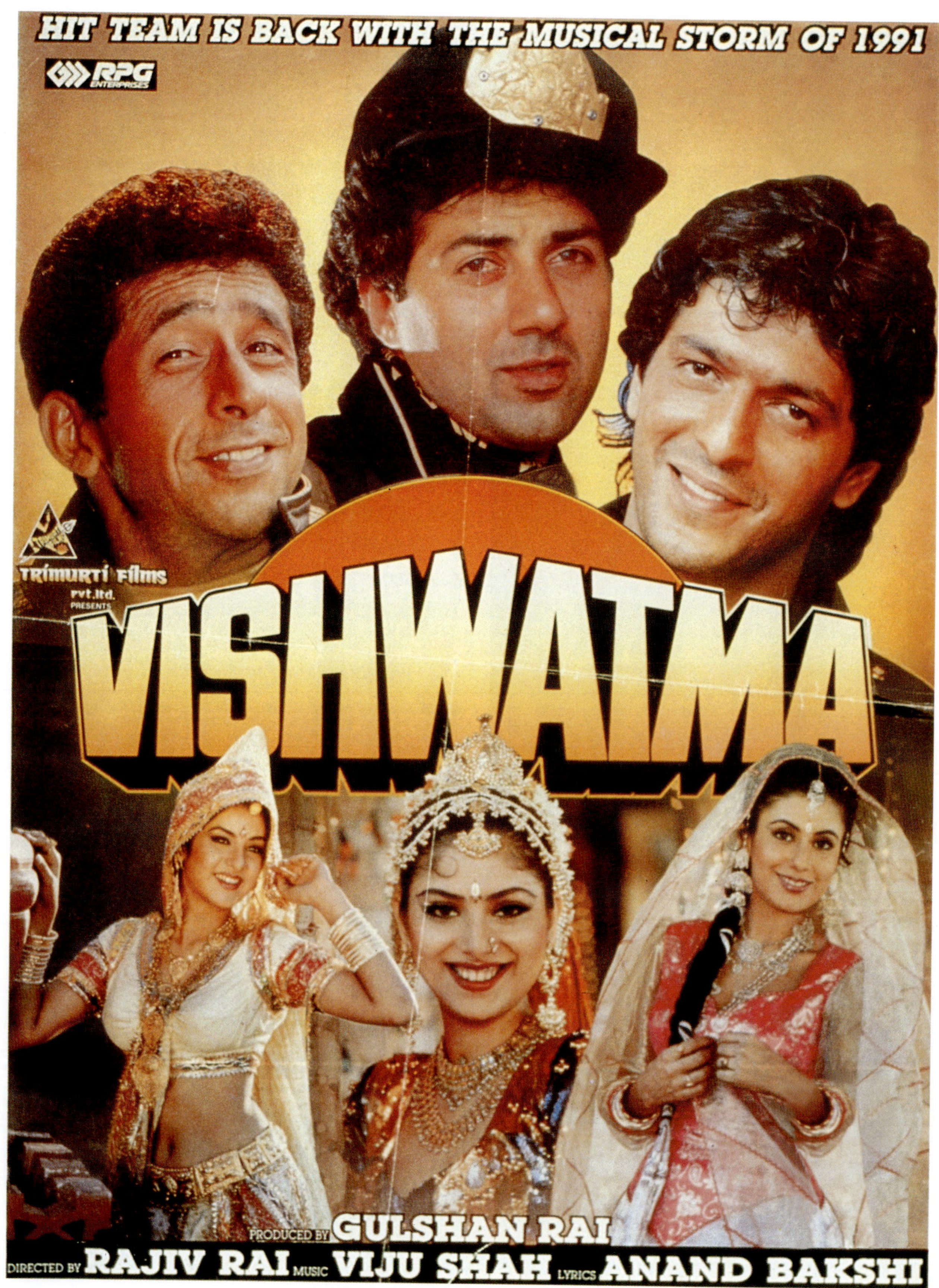
HIT TEAM IS BACK WITH THE MUSICAL STORM OF 1991
RPG ENTERPRISES
TRIMURTI FILMS
PVT.LTD.
PRESENTS
VISHWATMA
PRODUCED BY GULSHAN RAI
DIRECTED BY RAJIV RAI MUSIC VIJU SHAH LYRICS ANAND BAKSHI

■ Indian film poster for the 1991 musical *Vishwatma*

gesture, and make it more than that—I have carved a space with it, made a shape with it, broken a shackle with it, freed a bird with it that has soared in countless imaginations. In my acting as in my life, I rode the stallion of time with the free rein of opportunity; and in so doing, I gave the ordinary people, the ones in the twenty-five paise seats, a truth more valuable than the tattered truths of their tawdry lives.

. . . So someone will find out how to stop the pain, someone will find out who did it, someone will arrest the villain for the crime, someone will find the lyrics to the theme song, someone will gather the crowds for a joyous celebration, and then, only then, as the flames flicker and the shadows dance and the people in the twenty-five paise seats applaud and whistle and the stories merge and melt and dissolve in the heat, only then will it be, only then can it be,

the end. ■

Excerpted from Shashi Tharoor, *Show Business: A Novel* (New York: Arcade Publishing, 1992). Reprinted with permission of the publisher.

■ Shashi Tharoor was born in London in 1956 and was brought up in Bombay and Calcutta. He took a doctorate from the Fletcher School of Law and Diplomacy, Tufts University, and since 1978 has worked for the United Nations, where he is currently involved in peace-keeping operations. His first novel, *The Great Indian Novel* (Penguin, 1989), won the Federation of Indian Publishers-*Hindustan Times* Literary Award (1989–90) and a 1990 Commonwealth Writers Prize. *Show Business* (Arcade, 1992) is his second novel.

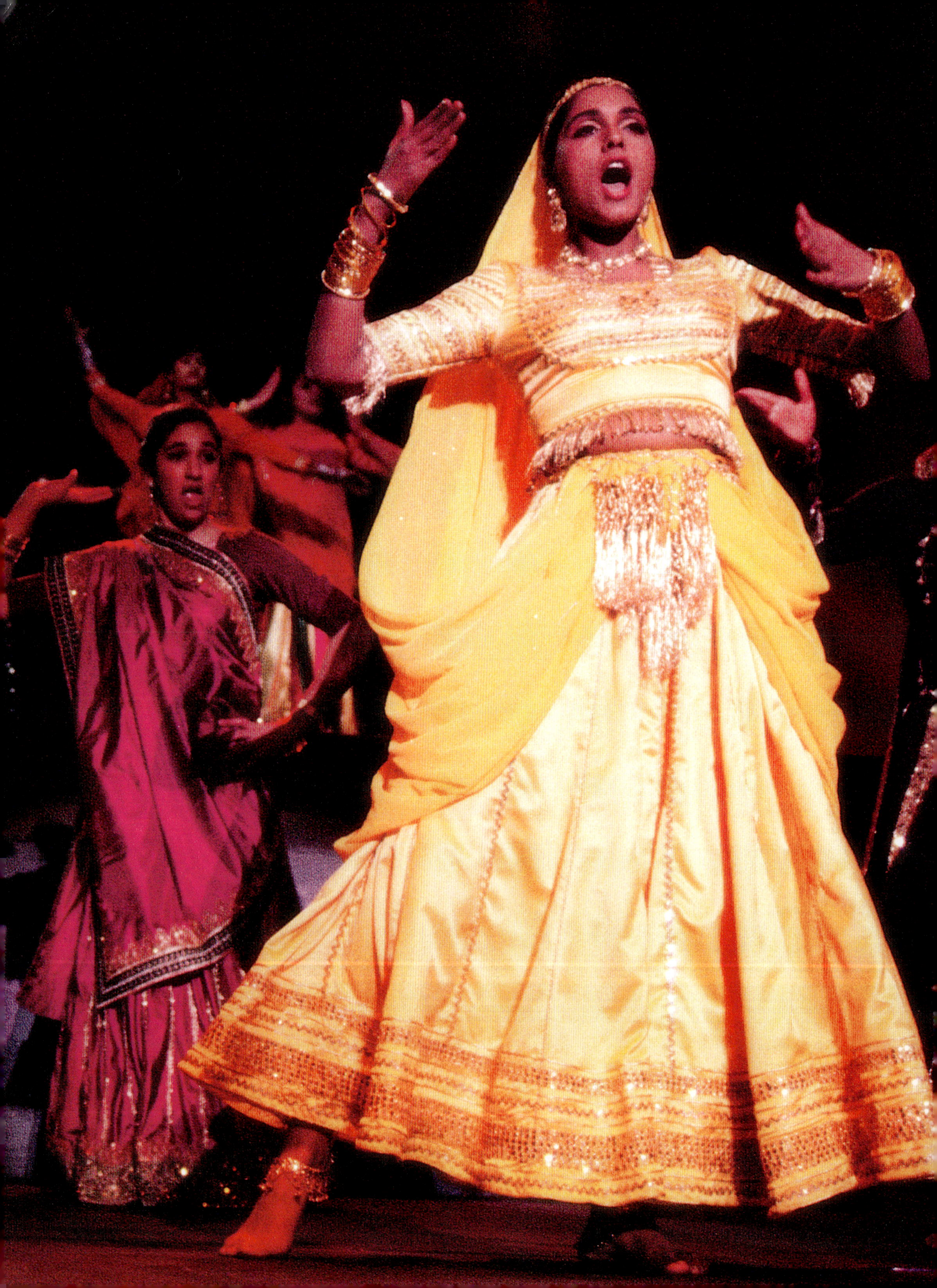

Film and Theater in India: A Sketch

The first film showing in India was on July 7, 1896, when the Lumiere Brothers displayed their "living photographic pictures" in Bombay—a few months after they had unveiled their invention to the world in Paris. The exhibition of Western films in India that followed this event used a medium that drew inspiration and form from the theater, as seen in the dramas, stagey in style, based on literary classics, and featuring well-known stars of the theater.

Indian cinema exhibited a close relationship to theater from the very beginning. Jamjetji Framji Madan (1856–1923), the pioneer exhibitor of films in India, was the owner of a theater company before he launched a "bioscope" show in 1902 in Calcutta.

Dadasaheb Phalke (1870–1944), widely regarded as the father of Indian cinema, was drawn to film through his interests in theater, photography, and magic. In choosing a story from the epic the *Mahabharata* for the first Indian film, *Rajah Harischandra* (1912), Phalke cannily tapped into a great oral tradition. The impact was enormous. Phalke went on to make more films based on Indian mythology, and it is said that people prostrated in the aisles when the god Rama appeared in Phalke's *Lanka Dahan* (The Burning of Lanka, 1917). Indian cinema had begun retelling and reinterpreting a mythology, traditionally passed down in oral, musical, and theatrical traditions, that had profound religious meaning for audiences, who were also familiar with the stories.

Ironically, while a great many early Indian films had religious themes, they still represented a process of secularization that had begun to sweep all aspects of Indian society. Until the advent of cinema, this process had been best expressed in the theater. The Indian film industry began in the cities of Calcutta, Madras, and Bombay, which enjoyed a rebirth of theater during the 1850s under the British. It has been observed that none of these cities—all seaports built by the British—had an Indian cultural history. Their history began with the coming of the British.

The middle class who led the revival of the new Indian theater in the nineteenth century based their productions on European models, adapting their plays from the European stage. In doing so, they introduced a new formal concept in Indian theater: the proscenium. The resulting separation of the audience from the stage had radical impact. The European models had distanced the performing art forms from associations with Indian rituals, but now the proscenium eliminated direct audience participation and minimized improvisation. Dissociated from the traditional functions of theater by the new middle class, theater became pure entertainment and the earnings at the box office emerged as the gauge for its success. No one had paid to see

■ Anu Agarwal, actress and dancer, performs at the Natraj Awards ceremony, New York, 1991.

the theater, or for that matter any of the other performing arts, since the presentations depended on the patronage of the local raja or temple. The secularization of entertainment resulted in theater as a packaged commodity to be sold over and over again.

With the coming of sound and the "talkie" in 1931, Indian cinema began to have an important and lasting impact on the performing arts of India. The first sound film was shown in India in 1929, and in 1931, *Alam Ara* (Beauty of the World), the first talking feature, was released. It was an overwhelming success. The new sound motion pictures conferred a status on vernacular languages—films were made in Hindi, Bengali, Tamil, Telugu, Gujarati, and Marathi in the first two years—in a country long dominated by the foreign languages of colonial powers. As an industry, it won government protection from competition by foreign films.

THEATER, MUSIC, AND FILM

The singularly Indian characteristic of the sound film in India was, of course, the use of music. *Alam Ara* had about a dozen songs and an early Tamil film reportedly had over sixty songs. Most also had dances. These "all-talking, all-singing, all-dancing" films had connected instantaneously with music-drama forms of traditional India, such as the *tamasha* of Western India or the *jatra* of Bengal in the east.

In doing so, Indian cinema joined a two-thousand-year-old tradition. In ancient India the idea of drama was not distinct from the perfoming arts of song, dance, and music. Indeed, Sanskrit and languages derived from it did not have separate terms for *drama* and *dance.* A performance was founded on the bedrock of music, which not only provided entertainment but also enhanced and underscored emotional continuity. When classical Sanskrit drama began its decline around A.D. 1,000, popular Indian drama survived as a folk form. To do so, it drew heavily from religious dance and drama in folk theater. Thus, song and dance were paramount in eliciting the mass adulation and popularity that Indian sound films enjoyed from the start.

While this tradition strengthened the Indian film, it had a negative impact on folk drama. This was especially true in the towns and cities where the cinema theaters existed. (Even today, Indian cinema is seen largely in urban areas.) The traveling itinerant cinemas—begun as early as when the pioneer Phalke traveled by bullock cart with projector, screen, and film—reached into the heartland of India. Film not only learned its tricks from the theater but produced cheaper made-to-order entertainment on a scale theater could not afford. Indian film almost completely wiped out the new middle-class theater. It is said that India has not seen professional theater of the same proportions since.

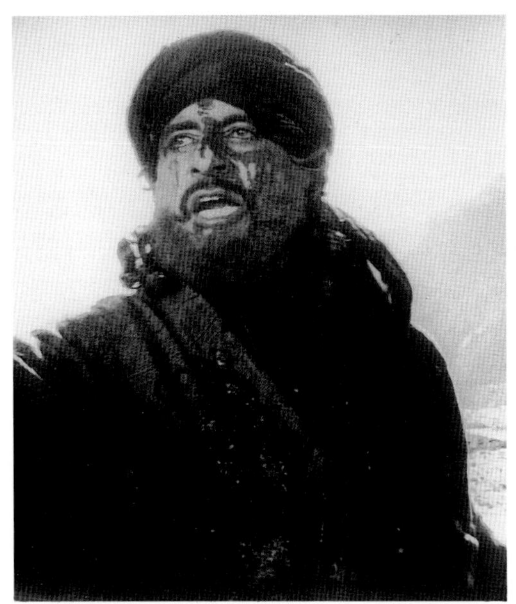

■ Amitabh Bachchan stars in *God Is My Witness* (1993).

The new theater had absorbed features of traditional or folk performing arts such as music and comic interludes, and these emerged as the distinctive stylistic characteristics of the Indian film. The importance given to music and the resulting formula film—with a requisite number of songs and dances—also resulted in less attention given to script values, especially after the 1940s.

Today, with only thirteen thousand cinemas, nine hundred films a year, and 850 million people, India has one of the lowest ratios of cinema seats to population. Power has shifted to the exhibitor and distributor who demand what they can sell: seven or eight songs, a few dances, and one or two big stars. All Bombay films are aimed at exploiting first the idolized stars, such as Amitabh Bachchan, some of them working on twenty movies at a time and often commanding half the total budget of a film. Singers who dub the songs for the heroes and heroines match the stars in determining the box-office success of the Indian film. Romance and action became the predominant subject, and the background and characters became increasingly glamorous. Film characters represent not complex psychological entities but ethical archetypes.

The ethnic and linguistic heterogeneity of the new entrepreneurial class producing films brought about the secularization of theater and also led to an absence of cultural specificities. Hindi, or more accurately, Hindustani, a mix of Hindi and Urdu, became the major language of the all-India cinema as the film industry became centered in Bombay, Madras, and Calcutta. Successful filmmakers made their films in Hindi, which did not have as extensive a literary background as languages such as Bengali, Marathi, and Tamil. But the diverse language map and market of India demanded concentration on Hindi, a sort of lingua franca, and this resulted in a rootlessness in Indian film.

The very character of the average Indian film is therefore deprived of true cultural moorings and devoid of the various regional and linguistic realities of India. Films became structured melodramas, with an emphasis on a superficial plot, an approach very different from traditional theater with its improvisation and cultural specificity. The enormous popularity of these films has then diminished the demand for the traditional performances, as the entire idea and context of entertainment have changed. ■

■ L. Somi Roy is a curator of Asian film. His film exhibitions have been shown at the Museum of Modern Art, the Asia Society, and the American Museum of the Moving Image, among others. He has written on Asian cinema for publications such as *Artforum* and *Cinemaya* and lives in New York City.

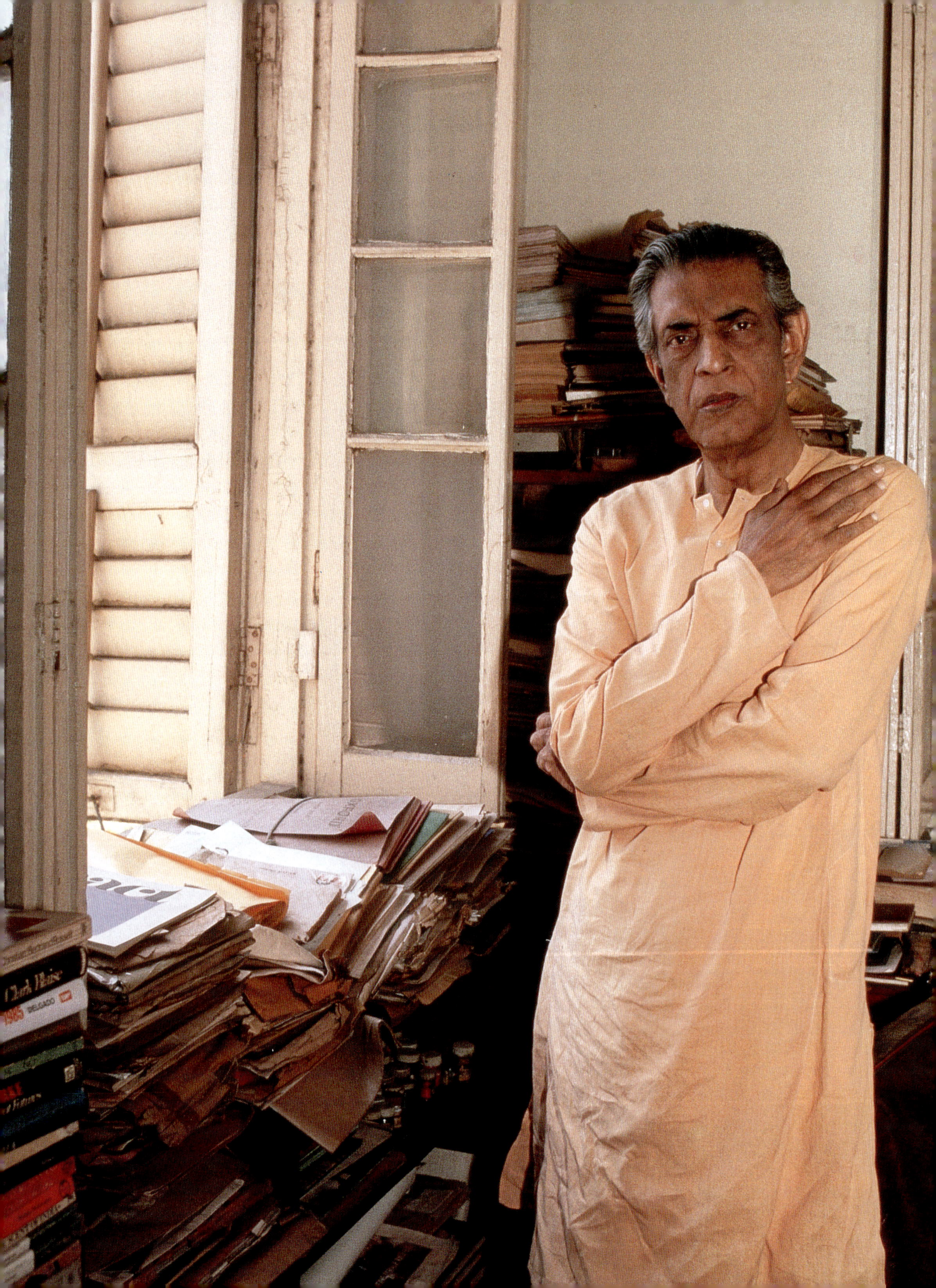
Clark Blaise
1985 DELGADO

RAGHUBIR SINGH

Photographs by Raghubir Singh

Satyajit Ray: From a Calcutta Room

Satyajit Ray lived in a sprawling flat, two flights up, in a colonial building in Calcutta. There his family still lives after the filmmaker's death, in late April 1992. There are two doors to the flat, and during Ray's lifetime, there were two kinds of visitors to the flat: the front door visitor and the back door visitor. The latter was almost always Bengali. Ray never came to the back door, but he almost always came to the front door, offering a characteristically limp handshake. During a conversation rarely lasting more than an hour, and more often less, Ray could be enthusiastic, friendly, and engaging, or he could be silent and polite—if the visitor put him off. His immense urbanity revealed itself even when he was angry or annoyed; he would only offer subtle hints that the visit was over.

Ray saw you either because he liked and respected you or because there was a purpose to the visit. In the latter case, you needed him, not vice versa. But every visitor, with few exceptions, left with the feeling that he had met true greatness—an artist who did not believe in compromise, who was incorruptible. A grand presence still pervades the room.

In 1980 an American photographer went to Ray's room. He had arrived in Calcutta after being, for twenty years, a Ray fan. He knew Ray's films. The maestro sensed that and responded with enthusiasm. But the photographer returned from the meeting angry and dissatisfied. He complained bitterly to me:

> Ray observes you all the time. Nothing escapes his notice. If you have a camera in your hands, his guard is up. He knows what you are going to do. The furniture is arranged to observe you: the light from two large windows falls on you, over his back. He sits on a high chair, you sit on a low one. With his height he looms over you. I could not get one good photograph.

Later, on the sets of *Pikoo* (1980), the American photographer was again unlucky. The set was very dark. Light fell on the actors, but not on Ray. In the darkness of the set, Ray with his head under the black cloth, his eye glued to the movie camera, caught the sound of the visitor's camera shutter and asked, "Is that a Leica you are using?" He appreciated the quiet shutter of the visitor's Leica, calling it "a gentlemanly sound." He knew the still photographer's art. He himself had been an avid photographer from his childhood to his early years of filmmaking. Therefore he could, with ease, anticipate the photographer's intention.

■ Satyajit Ray at home, 1991

Yet I could not agree with all the observations of the American photographer.

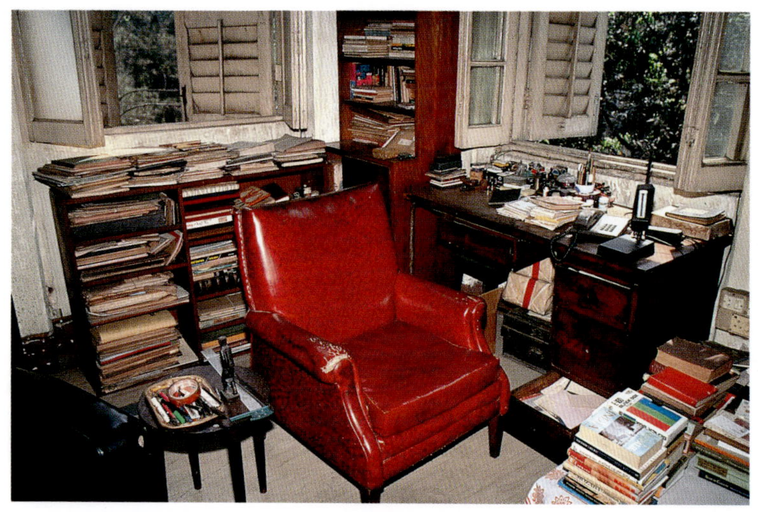

■ Satyajit Ray's chair, 1993

The furniture was not purposely arranged to study the visitor. Ray needed the high chair because he was six feet four inches in height. "I am the tallest man in Bengal," he once joked. He needed the light to fall over his shoulder while he sketched, wrote stories and scenarios, or typed letters with the machine perched on his lap, his long legs propped up against a cluttered table or equally cluttered settee. Yet it is true that Ray was an acute observer. His films are a testament to his sharpness of sight and sensibility.

In the "boxing match with time" (Henri Cartier-Bresson's definition of photography), in the observant camera of Ray's mind, Ray was the photographer and the visitor was the subject. When Ray left his room to work, on a location or on a set, the visitor had a better chance to observe Ray—while the director was absorbed in filming. Yet, in spite of being absorbed, the maestro was aware of the musicality of the world. He had his ear tuned to the goings-on around him, catching the softest of sounds: like that of the Leica shutter.

That is why I wonder how photographer Richard Avedon, an antihumanist artist, would have fared if Ray had allowed him into his room. "Avedon has sent me a huge cake," exclaimed Ray, in New York, in 1981. "He has been writing to me in Calcutta. 'Give me one month's notice,' he says. 'I will fly to Calcutta on any day of your choice.'" But Ray never allowed Avedon into his room. "I belong to the Cartier-Bresson school," Ray often declared.

Ray's films are also a testament to his deep humanism. That is why he fervently admired the work of Henri Cartier-Bresson. But Cartier-Bresson has considered himself a surrealist, while Ray disdained surrealism. Once when I mentioned Cartier-Bresson as a surrealist to Ray, he was alarmed. He relaxed and nodded in affirmation only when I added that Cartier-Bresson saw surrealism not as an imaginative artifice but as it manifests itself in daily life. Ray was a humanist in an antihumanist world. He prized psychology but not psychiatry.

While Ray was often guarded about his front-door visitors, he could be casual and accommodating to many of his back-door visitors. Those who came in through the back door were almost without exception Bengalis. Apart from the film stars and relatives who floated in with ease, they were Bengalis who wanted something. More than the front-door visitor, these back-door visitors needed Ray. They were willing to wait for hours, days, and even years, if necessary, to become a part of Ray's world. They became errand boys, assistants, managers, and in some cases even jesters of sorts. Seeing this procession of people entering through the back door and waiting in an anteroom, an old friend of Ray's once quipped, "Nothing grows under a giant banyan tree."

Indeed, Ray was both the giant banyan tree and the great storyteller under that tree. What happened around the "banyan tree" was of great interest to the clannish society that is Bengali Calcutta—Ray was a central person in that society. After each visit to Ray and his room, a blow-by-blow account would be circulated in certain sections of Calcutta. This close-knit society explains why Ray was cautious and reserved and why his attempts to guard his privacy failed.

By the late 1960s, Ray had given up walking the streets of Calcutta, stopping at pavement bookstalls and magazine stands, as he once did. He also gave up visiting the coffeehouse on Central Avenue, his onetime haunt. By 1970 he had shut himself in his flat—in his room—venturing out only by car. After his heart bypass operation he exercised by pacing up and down the small veranda of his flat. He could not take

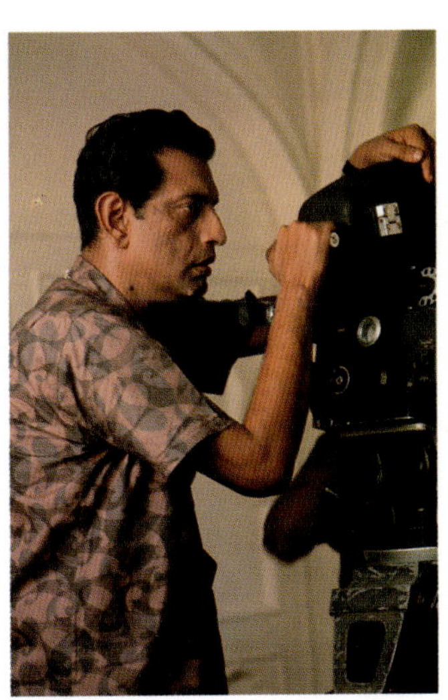

■ Satyajit Ray, 1968

SATYAJIT RAY

Best known as a filmmaker, Satyajit Ray was also a composer, a graphic artist, a designer of typefaces, an illustrator, a writer of children's stories and science fiction, and a winner of prizes in all these fields. He was born in 1921 in Calcutta to a family of distinguished writers, singers, and teachers. After graduating with honors from the University of Calcutta, where he majored in economics and minored in physics, he studied painting at Visva-Bharati University, but his hobby was going to the movies. As a layout artist and then art director for a British advertising agency, he continued to pursue his passion, and after seeing Vittorio de Sica's *Bicycle Thieves,* he determined to make movies himself. Borrowing money and pawning his wife's jewelry, he began to shoot *Pather Panchali* (Song of the Road) on weekends. With a grant from the West Bengali government, the film was completed in 1955. It played to full houses, and Ray became a full-time filmmaker.

There followed more than thirty films evoking the milieu of Ray's Bengal and twice that many awards from India and around the world. In 1992, shortly before he died, Ray received top Indian awards for his last film, *Agantuk* (The Stranger, 1991); India's highest civilian award, the Bharat Ratna; and an Oscar for Lifetime Achievement.

Sources: *Satyajit Ray: An Anthology of Statements on Ray and by Ray* (Bombay: Tata Press, for the Directorate of Film Festivals, Ministry of Information and Broadcasting, 1981); Peter B. Flint, "Satyajit Ray, 70, Cinematic Poet, Dies," *New York Times,* April 24, 1992.

■ Ray in his room, 1991

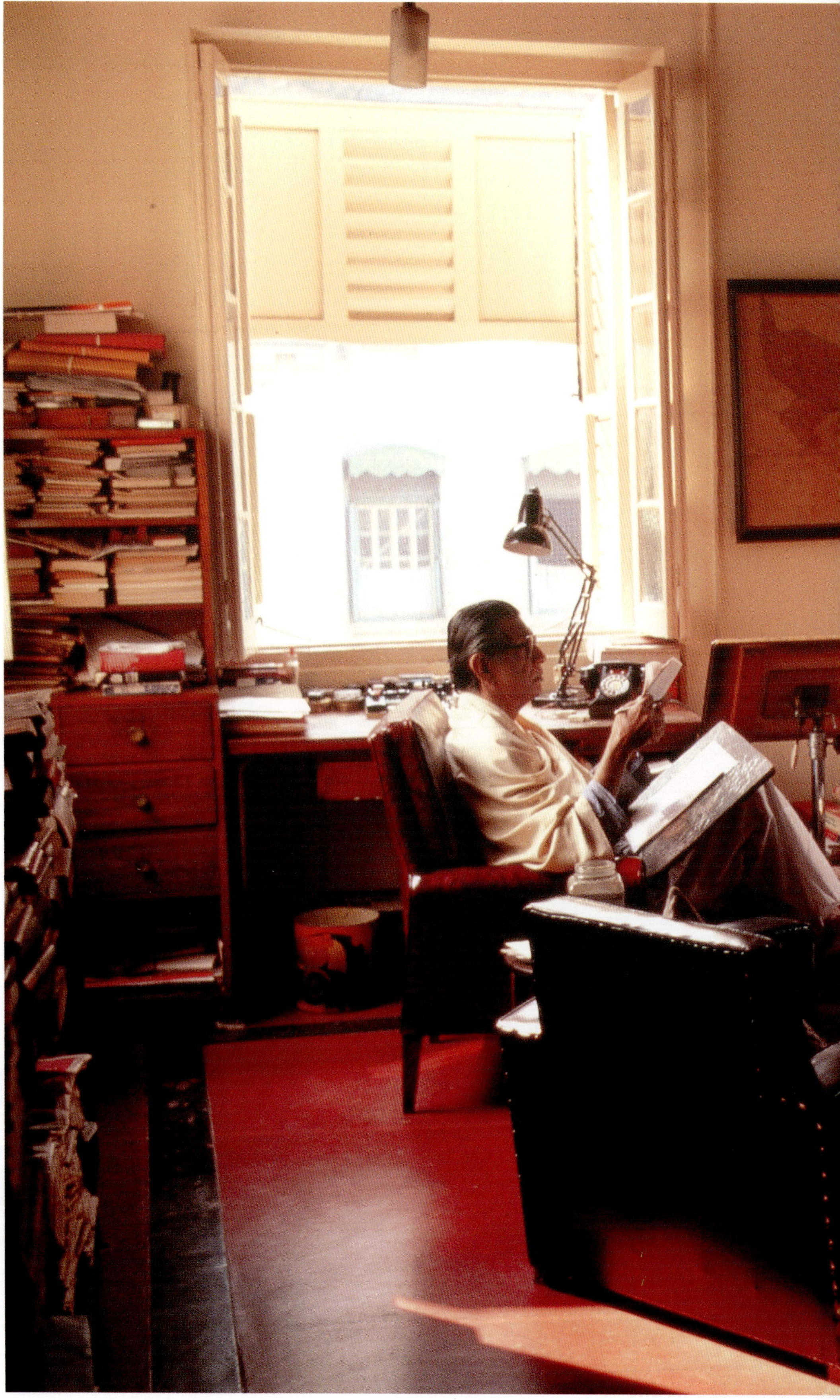

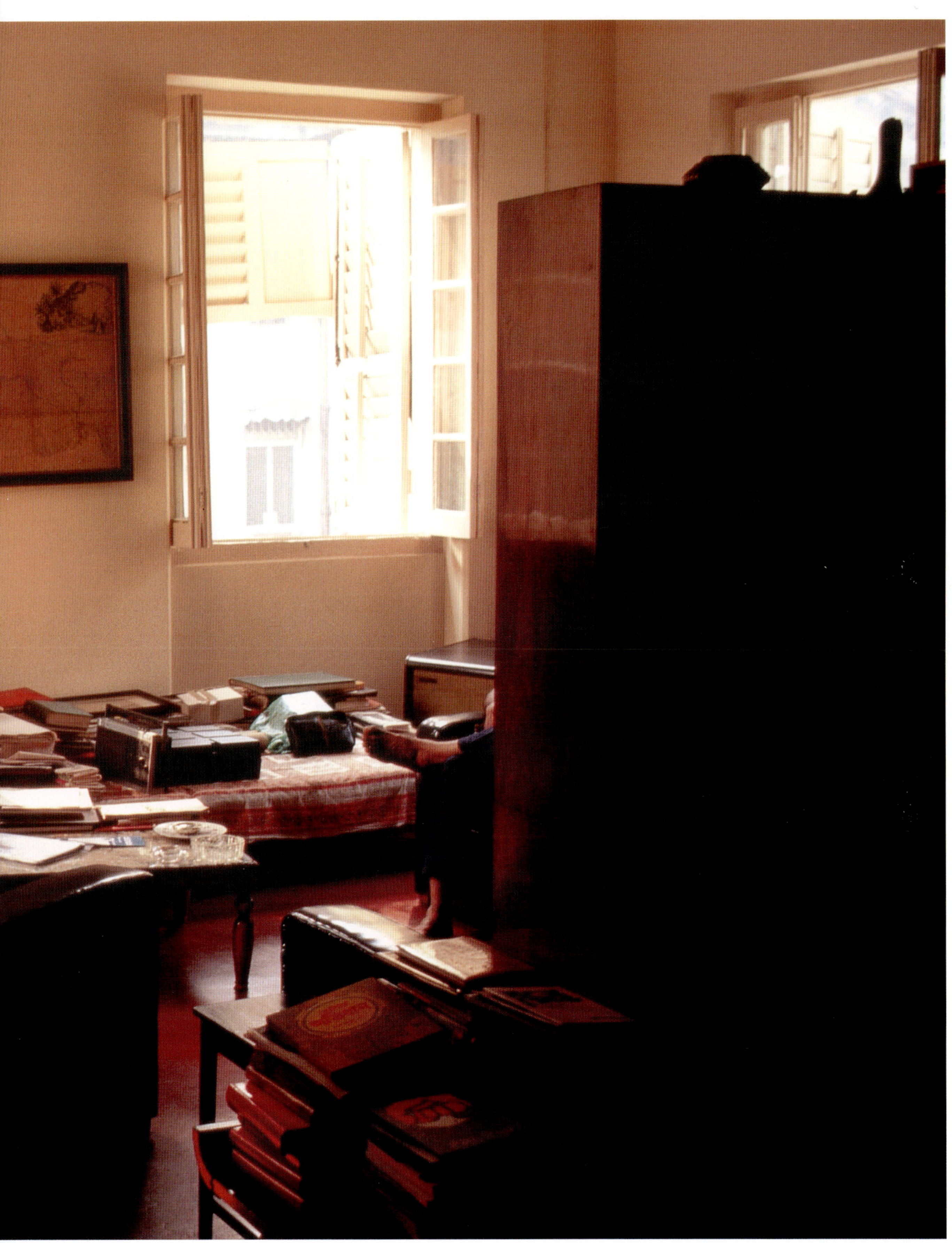

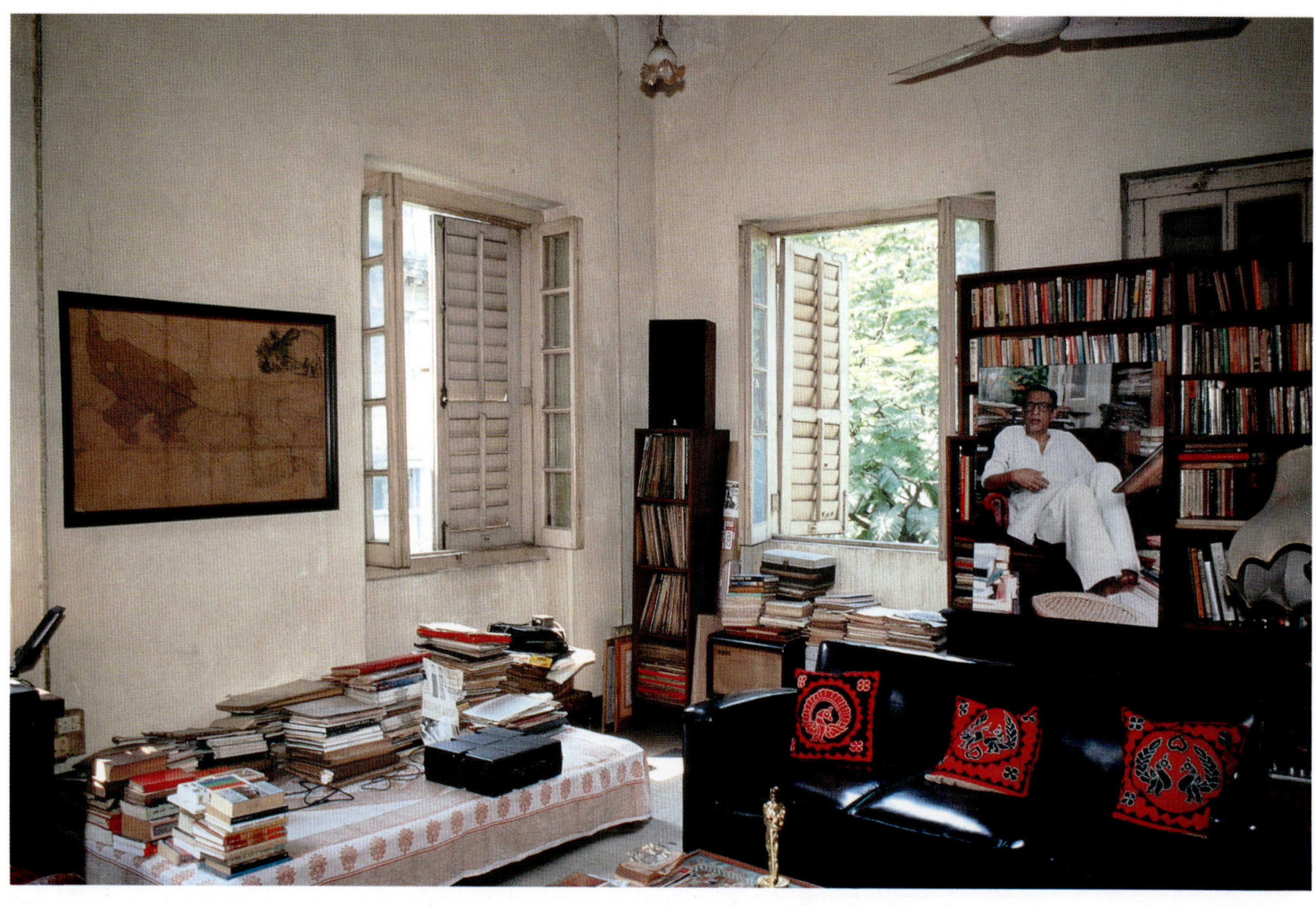

■ Ray's room, 1993

his daily walk in a public park. Bengalis, like most Indians, have no respect for privacy. He was their great artist and their only international legend. They wanted to look into his world. They wanted to touch him if possible or, failing that, at least come physically close to him—not knowing that he hated physical contact.

When François Mitterrand visited Calcutta in 1987, he awarded the Chevalier de la Legion d'Honneur to Ray. It is the highest award France gives to a foreigner. At the ceremony, after putting the ribbon with the medal around Ray's neck, Mitterrand, in Gallic fashion, attempted to embrace Ray. The maestro raised his arms to stop Mitterrand and then checked himself. The comic element of the scene was accentuated because Mitterrand, a small man, was dwarfed by Ray.

That gathering said much about Ray. Mitterrand had brought with him Jacques Lang, Jacques Cousteau, Maurice Herzog, and several other noted Frenchmen. The world came to Ray—usually to his room. He did not go to it. He kept in touch with it, through reading, through television, and by listening to and observing the visitors from all over the world who regularly visited him.

In twenty-five years of regular visits to Calcutta, and to Satyajit Ray and his room, I had come to know the filmmaker. Not only Ray and his work, but the room itself had become a presence in my mind. Therefore, one year after his death,

I went again to Ray's room. Now the front door to the flat is permanently closed. All visitors enter through the back door. Sandip Ray is the maestro's sole issue. His room, where most back-door visitors hung about during Ray's lifetime, is now the main room in the flat.

Ray's own room is little used, and then, it is with reverence. And only a gloomy corner is used, a dark corner created by tall bookshelves that act as partitions and block the light from the windows on the three opposite sides of the room.

A large photo-portrait of Ray dominates the main part of the room. The light from two sets of windows falls on the picture. The picture, propped up on a bookshelf, faces the now-empty wine red chair from which Ray observed his visitors. It is as if the presence of Ray in the picture is observing the space where he once sat and worked. No one except Shorodip, his three-year-old grandson, dares to sit on Ray's chair.

Ray's austere personality pervades the room. In contrast to most Indian homes, where the dead are venerated through photo-portraits garlanded by marigolds, with incense sticks stuck in cracks of the frame or held up in holders, Ray's picture is without any sentimental trappings. He is quite alone in his room.

A silence pervades the room; it is the silence of the opening sequence of *Jalsaghar* (The Music Room, 1958).

Like a cinema camera doing a pan, my eyes move from the closed front door to the windows at the other end of the room to take in many, many details: the old and dusty volumes of *Encyclopaedia Britannica;* books on cinema, art, science, design, music, history, theater, dance, typography, and photography; novels in Bengali and English. On top of the black piano on which he composed music, there is a picture of Sergei Eisenstein. Past the piano, after more bookshelves, there is Ray's wine red chair. On one side of it, there is a small table with a roll of transparent tape, a ruler, paintbrushes, pencils, pens, and crayons; on the other side there is a desk with a table lamp and a telephone. On the living room table and on the settee, there are stacks of books and magazines—V. S. Naipaul's last book on India is on top of a pile—near a book on Mozart. There are long-playing records on a shelf. There is a hi-fi music system. Above the settee hangs a large, antiquarian British map of Bengal. The room is a world by itself.

Then Bijoya Ray, his widow—the great woman behind the great man—her eyes moist with emotion, carries in the Oscar Lifetime Achievement Award. The gleaming statue is in contrast to the frayed and dusty trappings of the room. She places it on the table. The awards, the scenarios, the scripts and letters and papers that once lay about the room are locked up now. The room does not have a lived-in feeling. It is tidier than I have ever seen it. It has become a family shrine. Solitude pervades the room, the solitude in which a great artist worked. Yet the small room is marked by a sense of intimacy. The sense of intimacy and the face-to-face human contact one got when one visited Ray in his room suggested the maestro's cinema, which he called "the intimate cinema: the cinema of mood and atmosphere rather than of grandeur and spectacle."[1]

Ray's view of the world from a Calcutta room has been vigorously attacked by some critics and filmmakers who say that Ray, in confining himself to his room, simultaneously cut himself off from the world. They say that Ray's best work was his early period and pastoral films and not his films on contemporary India.

But the truth is quite different. What the act of confining himself to his room did for Ray was to reinforce his natural personality—his aloofness-cum-sense-of-observation. It gave him artistic distance. It was with a delicious sense of distance, and yet with complete intimacy and detail, that Ray viewed contemporary India. From his room Ray observed the world. He was that exceptional artist who could do that. In doing that he surpassed all the pamphleteering and activist and Marxist filmmakers of India. Ray had taken Jean Renoir's advice seriously. They first met in 1949, when Renoir filmed *The River* around Calcutta. Renoir told Ray: "You don't have to show many things in a film, but you have to be very careful to show only the right things." Much later, in Renoir's last years of life, Ray met him again in California. There Renoir suggested: "Let us spend an afternoon doing nothing." Renoir and Ray could make their films out of *nothing,* yet those nothings in their films are the most essential parts: they contain the human essence. In pursuing the human essence, Ray revealed his approach: "I still believe in the individual and in personal concepts rather than broad ideology, which keeps changing all the time."[2] Yet, however deeply he probed the human essence through his intimate cinema, he always maintained that delicious sense of distance. From the confines of his room, Ray touched the pulse of India.

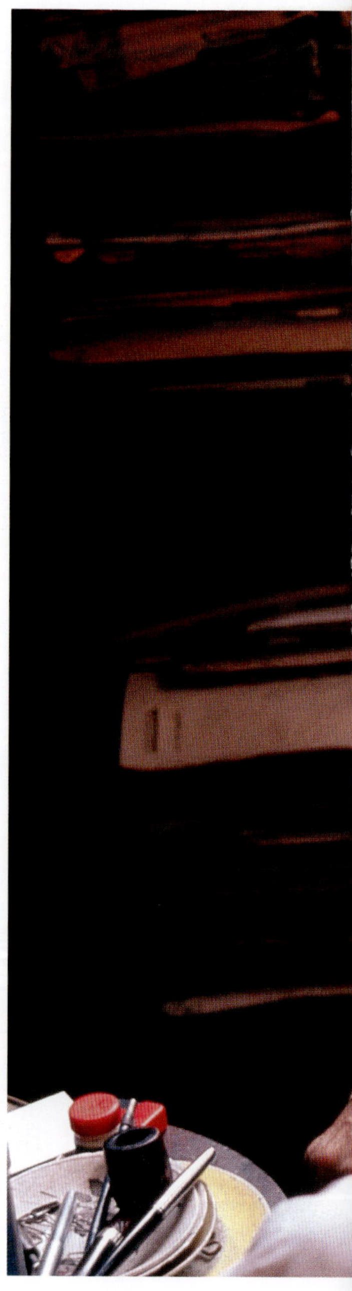

On a visit to Ray and his room in 1969, when refugees from East Bengal had begun to flood Calcutta and when the Naxalites (Maoists) were terrorizing the city and the state, I asked Ray if he intended to shoot a film relating to the harrowing events in Bengal. "I don't have a story," he replied thoughtfully. The following year he found one and filmed *Pratidwandi* (The Adversary, 1970).

Unlike the activist filmmakers and critics—people in a hurry—Ray took his time. Between 1963 and 1992, when he died, he had filmed thirteen stories on contemporary and postindependence India. In these films, the moral condition of changing India is laid bare through individuals, and a world of women and children is revealed.

So sure was Ray of his stance, so thorough was his preparation, that while filming in his psychologically complex but simple style, he acted swiftly and surely. He could finish filming a story in four to six weeks. He rarely did more than three takes; more often he was satisfied with one take, even with faulty equipment.

■ Ray at home, 1991

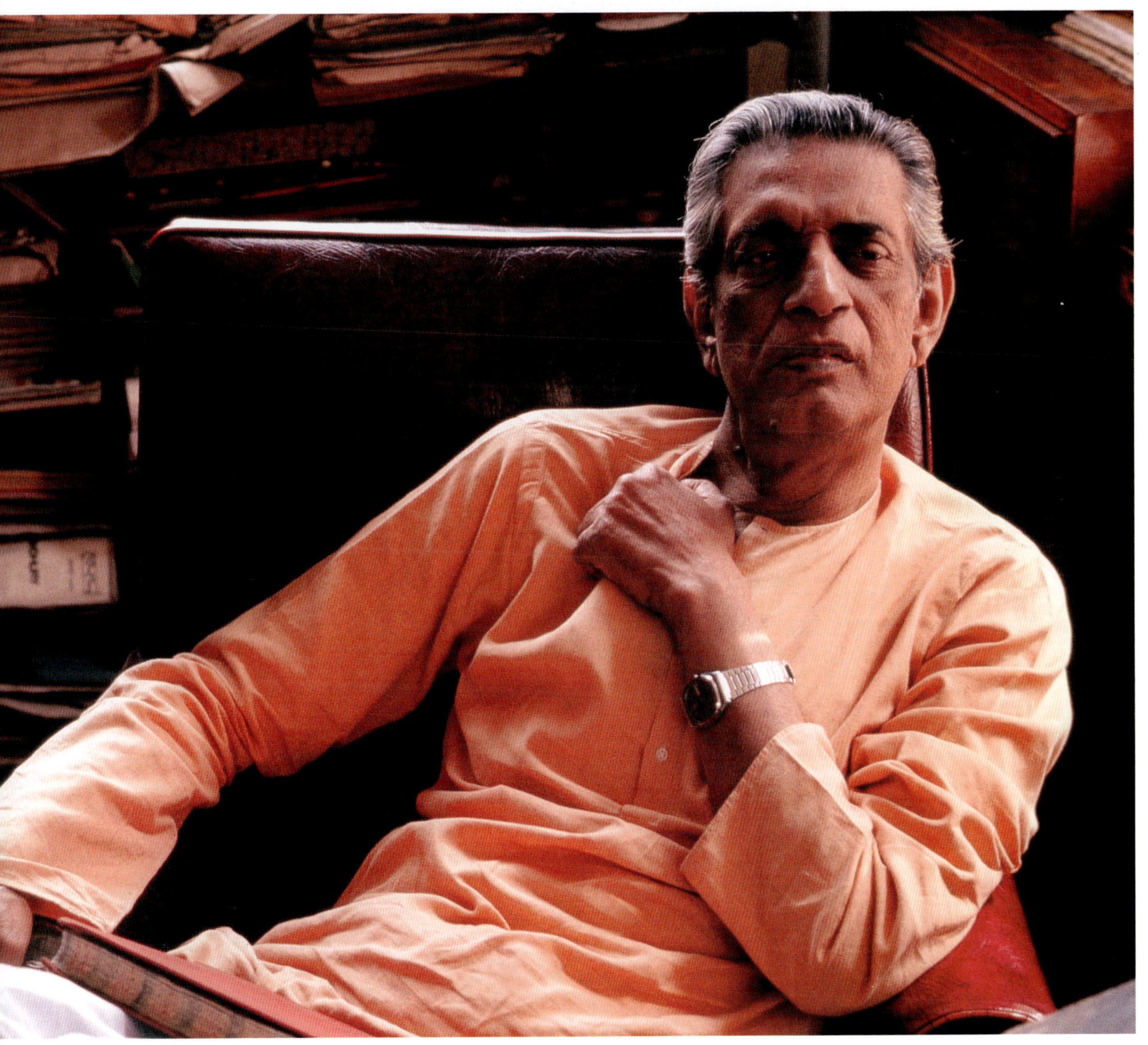

■ Ray's working conditions on the set for *Ganashatru* (Enemy of the People) 1987

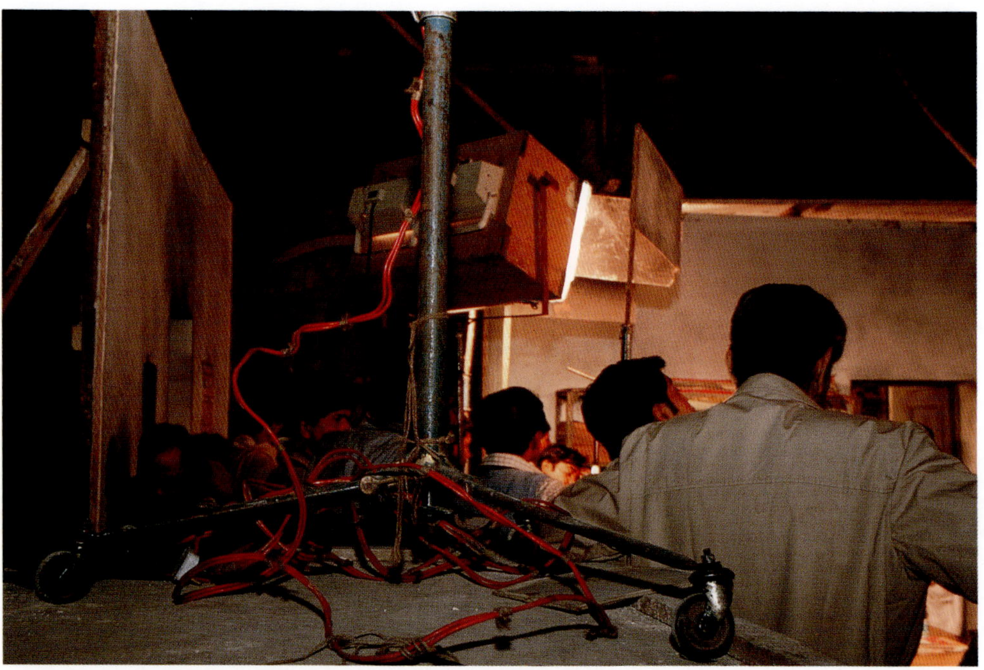

Nowhere in the world have so many masterly films been made with so little. Here is Ray on his filming conditions:

> The studios in Calcutta show their hallowed past in every crevice on the wall, in every tatter on the canvas that covers the ceiling. Some of the families of rodents that inhabit the rafters have lived there ever since the foundation of the industry. The floor is pitted, the camera groans as it turns, the voltage begins to drop after sundown. The general air of shabbiness is unnerving. And yet I do not mind these at all. I do not think of these as hindrances. After all, we have the essentials to make a film, and it is within us to make it badly or well. It is the bareness of means that forces us to be economical and inventive, and prevents us from turning craftsmanship into an end in itself. And there is something about creating beauty in the circumstances of shoddiness and privation that is truly exciting.[3]

If these conditions were restricting, they were nothing when compared to what would follow his heart attacks and bypass operation. In his final two films the doctors eventually allowed the scantiest of outdoor filming. Because Ray had mastered cinema, he rose to the new challenge of filming indoors. His room and his confined life had become metaphors for a new style. Although his filming had become as restricted as his life, *Shakha Proshakha* (Branches of the Tree, 1990) and *Agantuk* (The Stranger, 1991) are widely acknowledged as among his best films. He had made the films out of "nothing."

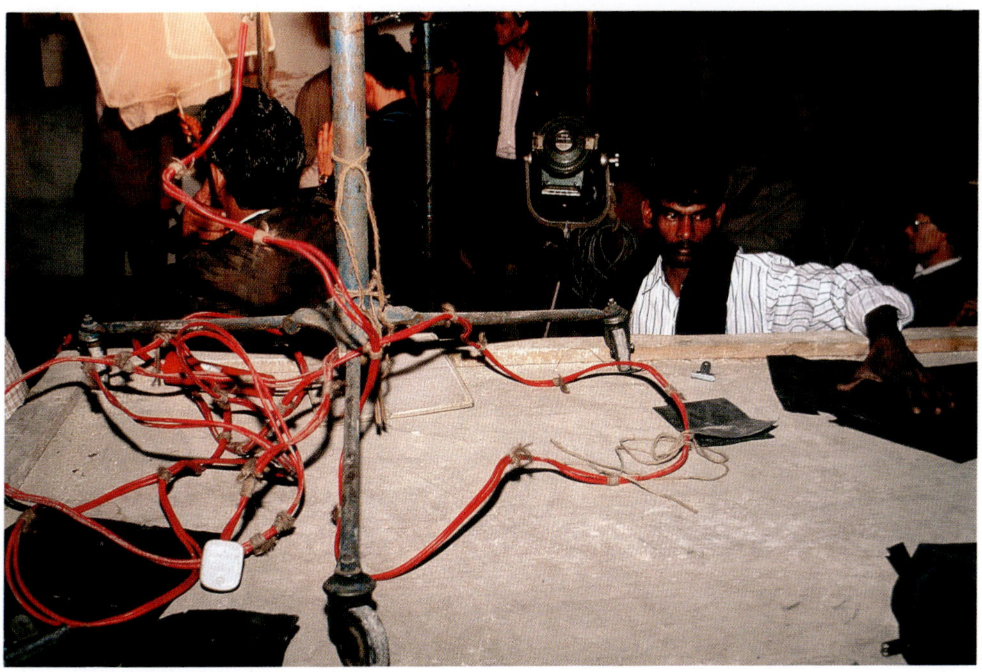

■ Ray's working conditions, 1989

Ray was planning yet another film when he died. He had written *The Broken Journey.* Sandip Ray, his talented son, has just filmed it. In this last story, Ray's own doctor is the model for the protagonist. Ray used his confined situation and the doctor's regular visits to his room to construct a moral tale: the smart city doctor's simple village encounters open a new world for him. We also realize how expensive lifesaving medicines are for the village dweller. From his first filmed story, the classic Apu trilogy, to his last written story, Ray, though a thoroughly urban and urbane man, remained in touch with the essential condition of India—the village. He had described his experience as "all middle class and that's rather a limited field,"[4] but a great and ruthlessly honest artist can rise above his or her limitations by knowing what those limitations are and by keeping a sharp eye and ear for the experience of others. Ray did that in his room.

Indeed, Ray from his room had much to teach India's filmmakers. He began early on as a film critic and rose to become the winner of an Oscar Lifetime Achievement award. After Ray won the Oscar, V. S. Naipaul, a fervent admirer of Ray, asked me, "Ray was such a grand man. Why was he so carried away by the Oscar?" I replied that when Ray declared that the Oscar was the greatest award he could receive, he was acknowledging his debt to Hollywood—the great Hollywood of John Ford, Orson Welles, Billy Wilder, and so many others.

As a young film critic in the 1940s, Ray had written a twelve-page letter to Wilder after seeing *Double Indemnity.* Wilder never replied. In 1962 when Ray was a noted filmmaker, he visited the sets of *Some Like It Hot* and was introduced to Wilder. Here is Ray's account of the meeting:

"You won a prize at Cannes? Well, I guess you're an artist. But I'm not. I'm just a commercial man, and I like it that way." I mumbled a protest. . . . But Wilder would have none of it. He just smiled and said: "Watch Lemmon do this scene. He's great"—and walked off. Thinking back on Wilder's remark now, I began to see the truth that it contained. If you have real talent and have found a break in Hollywood, and wish to keep going, it may be best not to talk about Art too much. What you have to try and do is keep your finger on the pulse of the public, your wits about you, and keep working. This is not easy but it has been done. . . . But this is rare in Hollywood.[5]

In 1992, during the Oscar awards ceremony in Hollywood, Wilder watched the video-recording from the Calcutta hospital where Ray, literally on his deathbed, gave a magnificent acceptance speech and mentioned that Wilder had never replied to the twelve-page letter. Just when Ray was breathing his last, Wilder sent a telegram to Ray:

> Dear Satyajit Ray so I did not answer to your 12 page letter. I beg your forgiveness and shame on me. But my congratulations on the well deserved Oscar. You are one of the greatest. Get well and come to see us. With respect and love.

According to Sandip Ray, who read this telegram to me, Ray had met with Wilder at Cannes in the early 1980s, and they had a long talk.

From Calcutta to California, Ray saw what he wanted to see of the world. I remember in Paris, in 1979, Ray was interested in seeing only what was new—the Centre Pompidou. He did not want to revisit any place he had already absorbed. His work in Paris over, he did not linger; he immediately flew back to his family, his work, and his wine red chair in the Calcutta apartment with two doors.

There in his dusty room, Ray worked with a probing eye for the cinematic dewdrop that reflected the human essence of the world around us. That dewdrop sparkled in the essential setting of India: the mountain, the river, and the plain—and the big city. In the big city it sparkled in the room with the two doors. ■

NOTES

1. Satyajit Ray, *Our Films, Their Films* (Calcutta: Orient Longman, 1976), p. 57.

2. Jean Renoir, quoted in ibid., p. 115; Ray, quoted in *Calcutta Financial Express,* April 26, 1992.

3. Ray, *Our Films, Their Films,* pp. 61–62.

4. Ray, quoted in *Calcutta Financial Express,* April 26, 1992.

5. Ray, *Our Films, Their Films.*

The River

It is the kind of cinema that flows with the serenity and nobility of a big river.
—Akira Kurosawa

It took me a long time to call him Manikda (literally, "jewel"), as many of his friends affectionately address him. From the mid-1960s to the early 1980s, I called him Mr. Ray. His Shakespearean actorlike presence, his commanding intensity flowing from his six feet four inch height, and the depth of his vision overwhelmed me. Appropriately, *Le Nouvel Observateur,* the French magazine, titled its story on Ray "Satyajit Rex." He is that. He is one of the emperors of international cinema.

Today, the emperor is in a Calcutta nursing home, fighting to live. Manikda's will to live was last revealed when he made three deeply felt feature films and one documentary film—after two heart attacks and a heart bypass operation. During the long recuperative period following the operation, there were whispers in India's film world that Ray's filming days were over. He surprised everyone by finishing these films—more work than many directors do in a lifetime. Appropriately, Nirad C. Chaudhari has said that only Satyajit Ray and himself have worked in Bengal. Even shorn of hyperbole, the statement has much truth in it.

For the film he was hoping to shoot last February, he had literally taken his doctor's stethoscope and touched it to the urban and rural world around him. In his original story—which he was casting when illness put him in an intensive care ward—a wealthy Calcutta doctor, who has rarely thought of rural India, makes a road trip to a small West Bengal town. En route, events force him to take a hard look at village India. In doing so, he learns—and we learn—how today's sophisticated but expensive medical care is out of the reach of the average villager.

Ray has always stood for the downtrodden and for women and children. His philosophy is humanity. Of course that does not satisfy the fashionable followers of Marxist and anti-Marxist philosophy. They ignore the fact that Ray's voice is the cinematically human voice of our age. His deep humanity has even touched Hollywood, which never made a penny from his films as it has from all the others who have been awarded the Oscar. That is the first of the two notable facts about Ray and the Oscar.

The second fact is the appreciation by slick Hollywood of a filmmaker from primitive Tollygunge, where in the rafters of the studios pigeons coo and deposit droppings amidst actors and directors. About these conditions, Ray himself has aired his feelings:

> One holds one's breath for fear the lights might go down in the middle of the shot, either of their own account or through a drop in the voltage; one holds

> one's breath while the camera rolls on the trolley, lest the wheels encounter a pothole on the studio floor and wobble . . . ; one holds one's breath on location in fear of a crowd emerging out of the blue . . . ; one holds one's breath while the film is processed for fear of its being spoiled through sheer carelessness; one holds one's breath too, while the film is being edited, because one never knows when the ravaged Moviola might turn back on the editor in revenge and rip the previous film to ribbons. No wonder filmmakers become prone to heart diseases. . . .

While the Oscar is a public tribute, Ray's seventieth birthday, exactly a year ago, brought deeply felt private tributes. These tributes are gathered together in a book (*Satyajit Ray at Seventy,* Eiffel Editions, Brussels) of photographs by Nemai Ghosh. This little-known book is valuable because of contributions by Michelangelo Antonioni, Akira Kurosawa, Martin Scorsese, and a variety of known and unknown persons. They raise a fundamental question: how do our tributes fare against the foreign ones? I am afraid our critics and commentators cannot express deep feelings directly and simply or put forward the kind of penetrating observations the foreigners have done collectively about our finest artist.

Here is Martin Scorsese:

> One of the great cinematic experiences of my life was in the early 1960s when I watched the complete Apu trilogy. . . . I was as totally absorbed as one would be reading a great epic novel. Satyajit Ray's ability to turn the particular into the universal was a revelation to me. . . . I then sought out other Ray films. . . . Ray's magic, the simple poetry of the images and their emotional impact will always stay with me.

Here is Antonioni: "My admiration for Satyajit Ray is total." Here is Jean-Claude Carriere, the noted scriptwriter of Peter Brook's *Mahabharat* and of Luis Buñuel films:

> I locked myself in a room to watch this unknown movie *Jalsaghar.* At some point, my wife came in and spoke to me. I didn't hear her, or even notice her—I was somewhere else. . . . Few films have fired me with such a transport of feeling.

Among the few fine Indian tributes, Madhabi Mukherjee's is deeply felt. "I was given rebirth by him in *Mahanagar*—a small window opened for me onto a vast world. I was a lump of clay from which he first sculpted an idol, then gifted it the power of vision." Another noted Ray performer, Soumitra Chatterjee, illuminates us

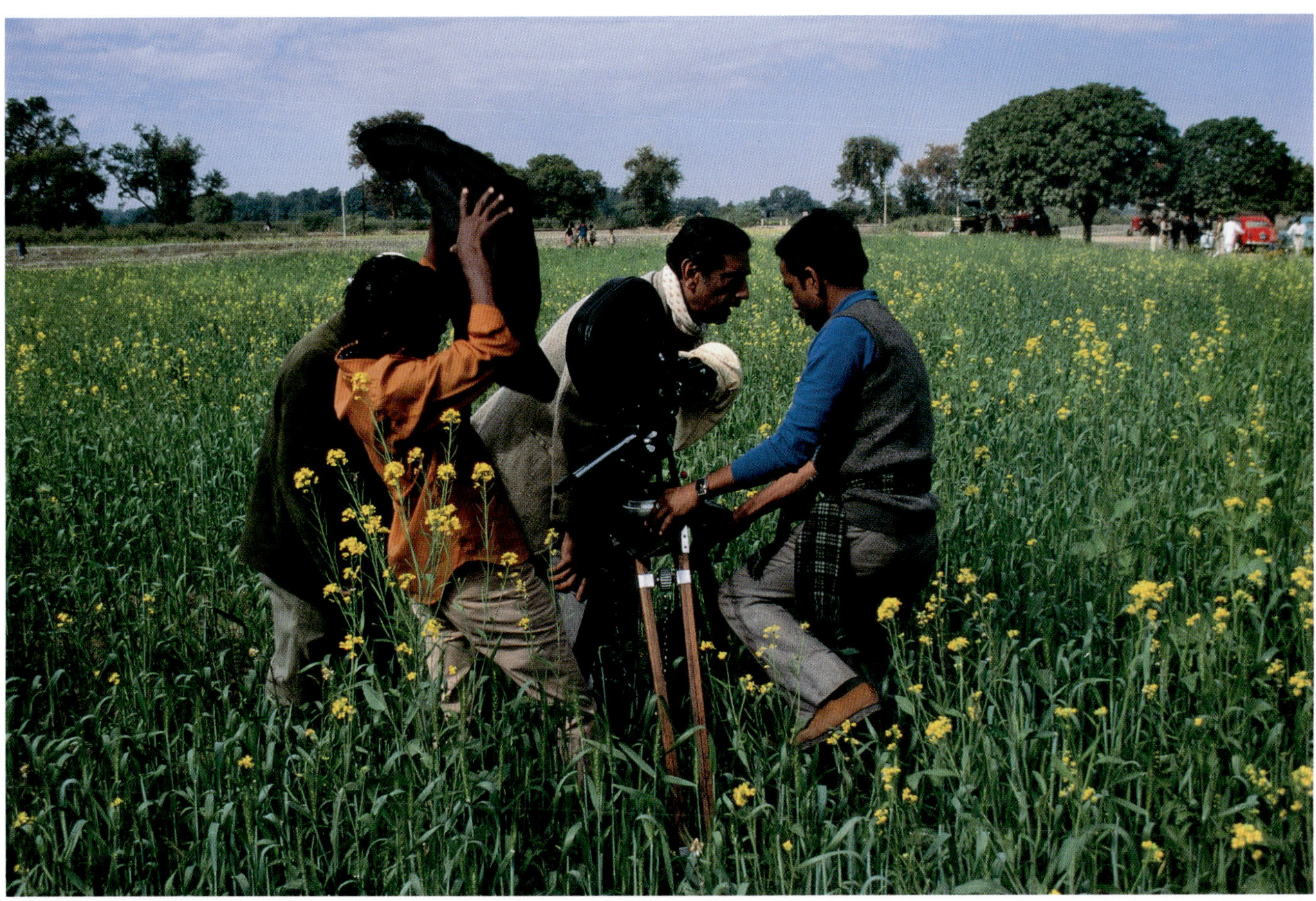

■ Ray filming *Shatranj Ke Khilari* (The Chess Players) in Lucknow

about acting for Ray: "I think the most important contribution an actor can make in a Ray film is to provide the character he is playing with an emotional authenticity."

Surprisingly, it is not the Indian film critics but the art historian Partha Mitter who reveals to us something of Ray's Mozartian sensibility. He writes:

> Ray spoke vividly of how Mozart (and Verdi) had solved the problem of treating a dramatic situation musically through the interplay of multiple concurrent vocal parts. What I did not realise then was the profoundly musical and even operatic nature of Ray's own sensibility. This has been borne out in all his films from *Pather Panchali* to his latest [this was written before *Agantuk*] one *Shakha Proshakha,* where he creates an interplay of characters through dialogue that is among his most imaginative, complex and powerful.

Ray himself has said that words can be visual. But he has also said, "The really crucial moments in a film should be wordless." There is no contradiction in these statements. They suggest the enormous canvas of Ray. He has created a whole cinematic body of sound and silence and another body of the mix of Western and Indian classical music.

Ray's is among the most musical of sensibilities in the whole history of cinema. He himself has observed:

> Films and music have so much in common! Both unfold over a period of time; both are concerned with pace and rhythm and contrast; both can be described in terms of mood—sad, cheerful, pensive, boisterous, tragic and jubilant. But this resemblance applies only to Western classical music. Since our music is improvised, its pattern and duration are flexible. . . . Also, the structure of Indian music is decorative, not dramatic. . . .

About the natural talent of Ray, Akira Kurosawa has said:

> Without the least effort and without sudden jerks, Ray paints his picture, but its effect on the audience is to stir up deep passions. How does he achieve this? There is nothing irrelevant or haphazard in his cinematographic technique. In that lies the secret of its excellence. . . .

. . . Ray saw things differently. He looked at the world through expressive personal psychology. This was an early lesson Ray had learned from Rabindranath Tagore. Tagore had written in Ray's diary that he had seen the world, he had seen all the rivers, he had seen all the mountains, but he had failed to see that dewdrop on the stalk of rice a few steps from home. Apart from its obvious meaning, this is a great lesson in India's sacred ecology. The ecology of India: the mountain, the river and the plain are among Ray's most eloquent characters. In his cinema, nature is stunning.

What distinguishes Ray and puts him alongside Jean Renoir—perhaps the director he most admired—and Chaplin and Eisenstein is his total psychology. Ray's psychological contact with people, with nature, with locale is unmatched. He is at his best when there is no dialogue and we view his pure and silent cinema. For these reasons, the layers of meaning, particularly of his contemporary cinema, are yet to be fully unraveled, to be fully appreciated. . . .

Ray's films, including his contemporary ones, are the works of a man of conscience, a man with a superlative sense of history. He is the cinematic-biographer-artist of our age. . . .

In creating his epic work which reveals a Mozartian as well as a *Mahabharat* sensibility—because his films have no real villains—Ray has fulfilled what a 1960s' *Time* magazine cover story on international cinema saw as his prodigious promise: will he be the Shakespeare of cinema?

The flowering of Ray's cinema is the last record of genius of the Bengal

■ Raghubir Singh was born in Jaipur in 1942 and has devoted his career to photographing his native India. He has also photographed in France, England, and Africa. He has had several one-person exhibitions in the United States and is the author of nine books, including *Rajasthan, India's Enchanted Land,* with a preface by Satyajit Ray (Thames and Hudson, 1981), *Kerala, Spice Coast of India* (Thames and Hudson, 1987), and *Calcutta, The Home and the Street* (Thames and Hudson, 1989). His most recent book of photographs is *The Ganges* (Aperture, 1992). *Bombay,* with a conversation with V. S. Naipaul, will be published by Aperture in late 1994. Raghubir Singh lives in London.

Renaissance. That age would have been alive today, if the Bengalis had paid equal attention to business as well as art, which the men and women of the Italian Renaissance did. That extraordinary oversight brought Bengal down. . . .

Yet, we must be thankful to Bengal that a cinematic river broke out from a stream—the Bengal Renaissance—and gave life to the infertile land of Indian cinema. Most of those who viewed the river of Ray were inspired, including—at last—Hollywood. ■

Excerpted from Raghubir Singh, "The River," *Sunday,* May 9, 1992, pp. 53–61.

FURTHER READING

Das Gupta, Chidananda. *The Cinema of Satyajit Ray.* New Delhi: Vikas, 1980.
A Bengali critic's assessment of Ray.

Ray, Satyajit. *Our Films, Their Films.* Calcutta: Orient Longman, 1976.
A collection of Ray's writings on Indian and Western cinema.

Robinson, Andrew. *Satyajit Ray: The Inner Eye.* Berkeley, Calif.: University of California Press, 1990.
The second English-language biography on Ray.

Rushdie, Salman. *Imaginary Homelands.* London: Viking Penguin, 1991.
Essays by Rushdie, with one on Ray, included in a review of Robinson's book.

Satyajit Ray: An Anthology of Statements on Ray and by Ray. Bombay: Tata Press, for the Directorate of Film Festivals, Ministry of Information and Broadcasting, 1981.
Summaries of the films, with comments by Ray and others.

Seton, Marie. *Portrait of a Director.* London: Dobson Books, 1971.
The first English-language biography of Ray.

Wood, Robin. *The Apu Trilogy.* New York: Praeger, 1971.
An assessment of Ray's first three films.

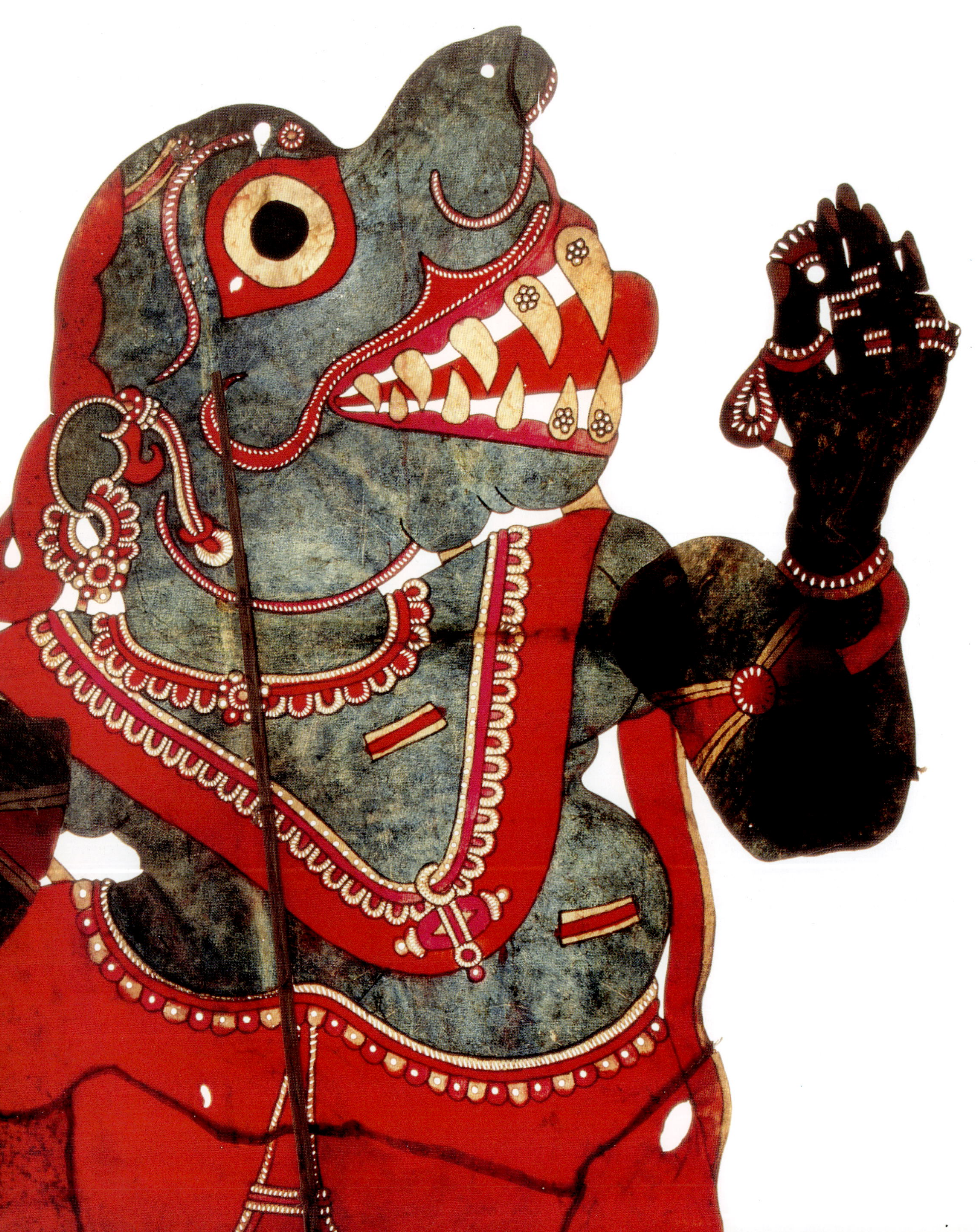

BRUCE ELLIOT TAPPER

Shadow Puppets of Andhra Pradesh

Many wandering entertainers and peddlers pass through an Indian village during the course of a year—offering to sing ballads, tell fortunes, sell amulets, perform acrobatics, charm snakes, weave fishnets, do tattoos, mend pots. It is an ancient custom by which—for centuries before radio, movies, and television—the knowledge of the Hindu epics and local folk tales, not to mention news, spread to the most remote corner of the subcontinent.

During the entire two years in the early 1970s that I lived in Yatapalem, part of the rural farming village of Aripaka about forty kilometers from the port city of Visakhapatnam in the Telugu-speaking state of Andhra Pradesh, not one of these was a troupe of shadow puppeteers. Intrigued by accounts of this traditional form of folk drama, I had hoped to see it at some time during the course of my doctoral research on society and ritual. The tradition was unique for producing puppets of individual characters as high as 175 centimeters. Occasionally I would ask villagers if shadow puppeteers ever came through the area. Those who knew what I was talking about said a troupe had not been heard of for at least five years.

Then one day my cook and assistant reported that he had heard of a troupe while shopping at the weekly market in Subbavaram some eight kilometers away. It had vanished by the time we arrived, but I was soon inspired by a book on the history of Telugu theater to visit the town of Srungavarapukota where it said a group of shadow puppeteers lived. I could find no trace of them. By a stroke of luck, the rickshaw driver I had engaged happened to come from a nearby village where a troupe of shadow players had performed about a week before. We set out on unpaved roads for several miles in the direction of the village and questioned passersby walking in the opposite direction. Some accounts conflicted. The explanation became apparent when the trail led to a troupe of marionette players. Marionette shows are called *bommalata* (puppet plays), while shadow plays are *tolubommalata* (leather puppet plays). We pushed on, following the other leads, and ultimately found them—a family sitting on mats encamped in the shade of a tree with their bundles of belongings and a packhorse.

They said they were members of the Sadra Bundali caste, based during the rainy season southwest down the Andhra coast in a town in the western part of the Godavari River delta. After considerable bargaining they consented to come to Yatapalem to give a performance the following week—for an amount in cash plus three measures of rice and a chicken. It was common for village residents to sponsor performances by traveling bards or performers for the entertainment of

■ Note: All the puppets depicted here were made by members of the Telaga Bondili caste in the Godavari delta region of Andhra Pradesh, India, and are in the collection of the author. They were acquired in 1972. Measurements are of height unless otherwise noted. The alternate names in parentheses are the Telugu names of these characters, which sometimes differ from the versions more commonly known in English.

■ Detail, Rakshasa. See page 57.

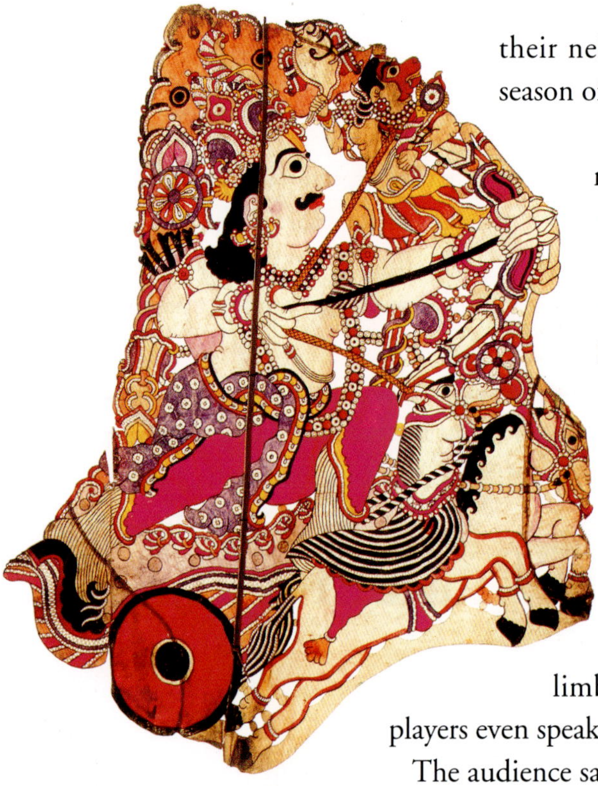

their neighbors, especially at that time in January, a postharvest season of fairs and festivals.

There was much excitement when the troupe arrived and borrowed clothes from the villagers to make the screen, formed by stretching two three-meter-long men's white dhoti cloths horizontally one above the other across a framework of bamboo constructed from materials rented from the villagers. The players used palm leaves to cover the back and sides of the boothlike structure, which was high enough to stand up in. A colored sari was stretched across the bottom to conceal the shadows and movements of the players. The three strips of cloth were attached with date palm thorns used like basting pins. The translucent cloth screen was constructed at a tilt with the bottom toward the players, which prevented the shadow puppets from sliding and kept the limbs of the figures flat on the screen. I later learned that the players even speak of the puppets "standing" on the screen.

The audience sat in front of the screen—women and children in front, men behind, overflowing the village lane. Behind the screen was a single electric bulb suspended overhead (in the past a kerosene pressure lamp had been used) to provide the light to transmit the colors and forms of the translucent shadow figures through the cloth, making them visible to the audience on the other side, which sees only the puppets and not the players.

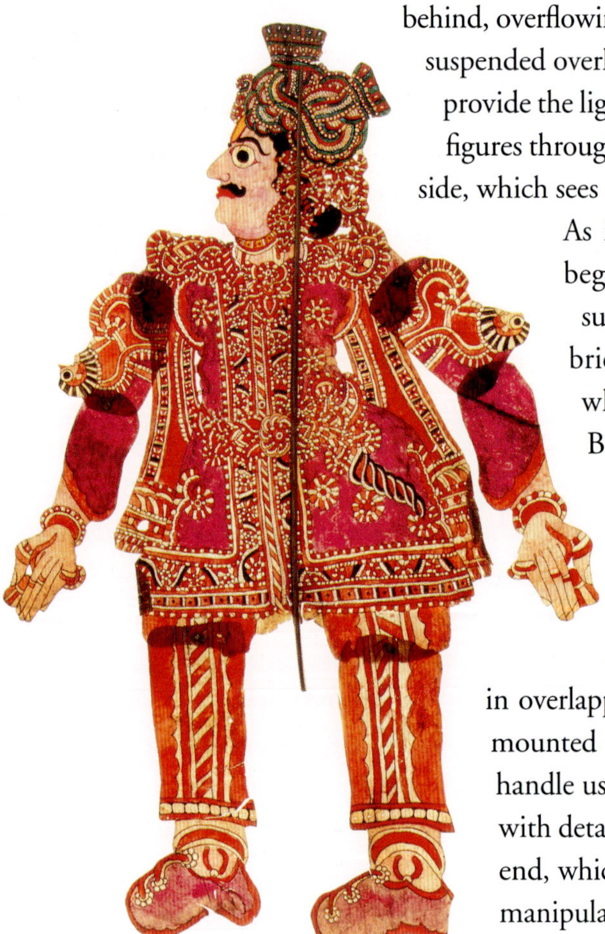

As is the custom for all village drama performances, this one began long after dark, around ten o'clock, and lasted until sunrise. The troupe knew its repertoire so well that it was only briefly before the performance began that the players asked which story to enact. I requested "Lankadahanam" (The Burning of Lanka), the well-known episode from the *Ramayana* of the abduction of Rama's wife Sita by the demon king Ravana. As with many stories popular locally, this was a tale of a wife's fidelity to her husband.

The performance began with a series of sung invocations and a line of ornate, strikingly stylized puppets pinned in overlapping fashion onto the sides of the screen. The puppets were mounted down the middle on a palm stem that extended to form a handle used to move the body of the puppet. Their arms were moved with detachable sticks that had a small piece of string with a peg at the end, which slipped into holes in the hands. Generally, one puppeteer manipulated all three sticks of a single puppet, holding the central

■ Arjuna (Arjunudu), one of the five Pandava brothers in the *Mahabharata* epic, 154 cm, parchment, ca. 1950s. His bow, quiver of arrows, and the unusual parrot design of his shoulder ornaments and bow handle are noteworthy.

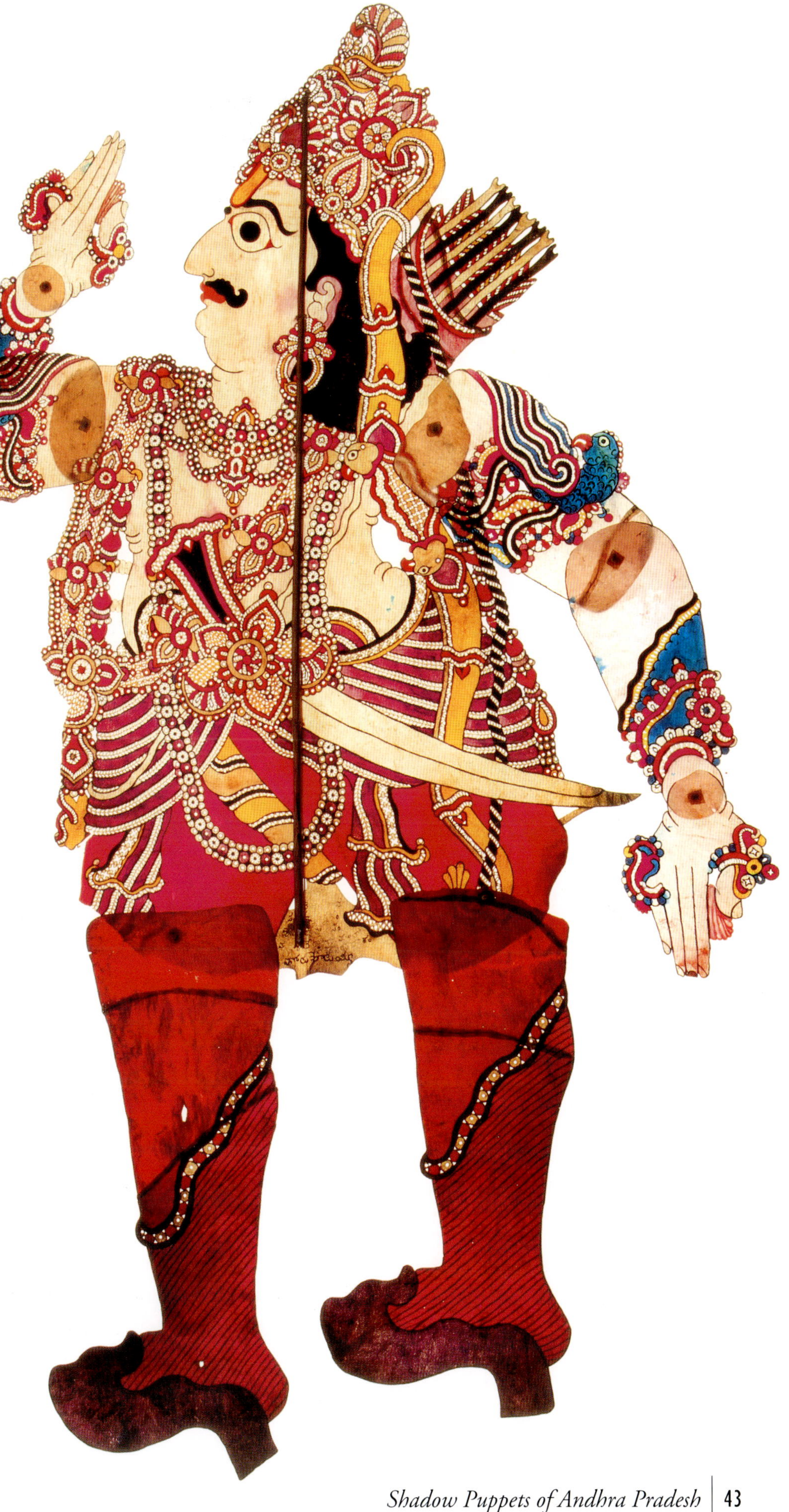

■ (Opposite, top) Arjuna going to battle in his war chariot, 105 cm, parchment, ca. 1950s. This puppet is a type used for battle scenes, depicting warriors on chariots with no movable limbs, and Arjuna's quiver of arrows and monkey standard are characteristic. Because this particular puppet is wider than most it is constructed with a jointed flap at the side to enable it to be folded for storage.

■ (Opposite, bottom) Saindava (Saindavudu), brother-in-law of Duryodhana, 154 cm, parchment, ca. 1950s. Curiously, this puppet does not have hands jointed separately from its forearms, and the leggings match the jacket.

■ Rama (Ramudu), 152 cm, parchment, ca. 1950s. Identified by the puppeteers as Rama, the hero of the *Ramayana* epic, this puppet can also represent Krishna, who features in the *Mahabharata* epic. Krishna is often associated with the peacock feather in his tiara.

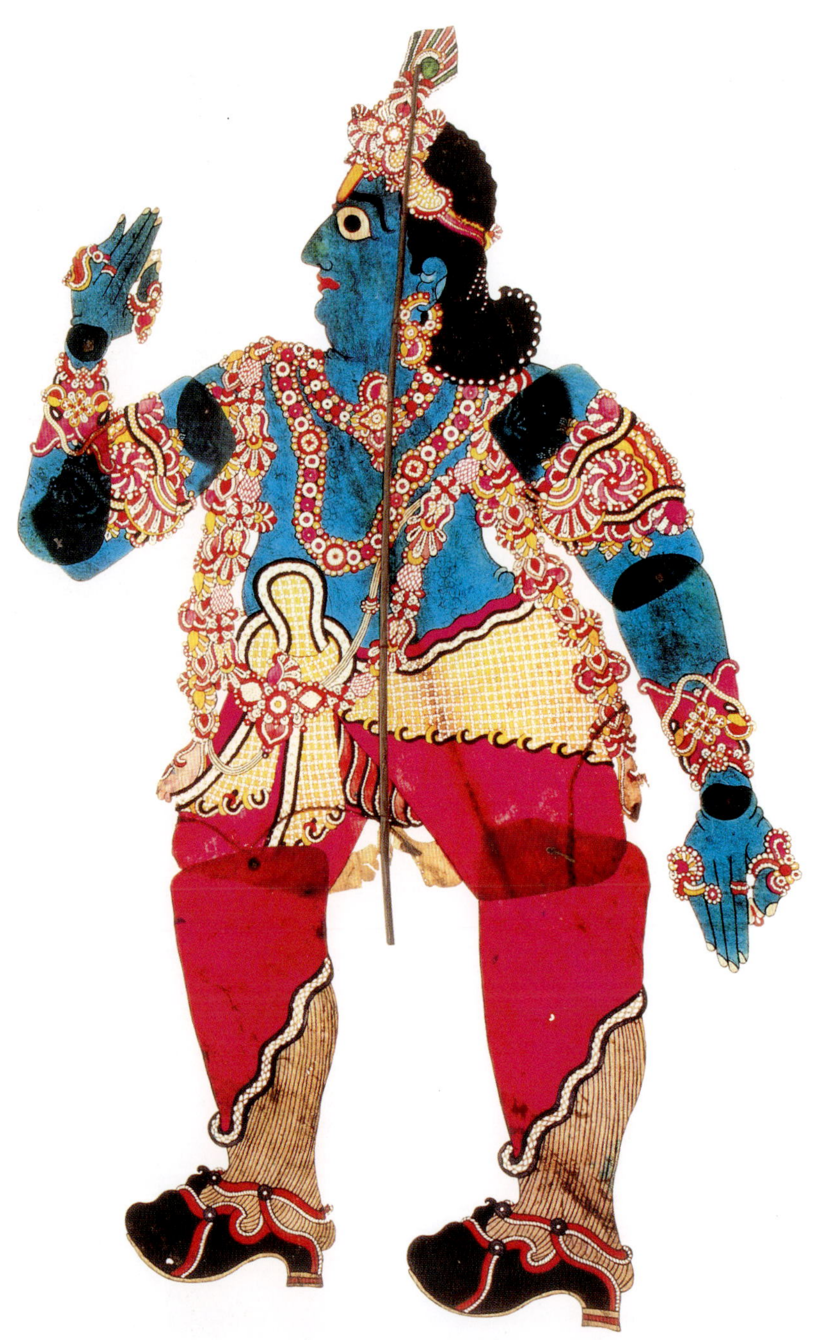

handle stick in one hand and the two arm-control sticks in the other. Often two to three puppeteers operated puppets on the screen at the same time, each one delivering the lines for his or her own puppet.

As the players manipulated the puppets, placing them on the screen and then moving them away, they created the illusion of the figures suddenly materializing and then fading out. They also caused the figures to walk, sway, hop, and fly through the air. The degree of skill they displayed in animating the dancers was astonishing. They would swivel a dancer's detachable head and manipulate her hands while

■ Jimutamallu, fighter for Duryodhana in the *Mahabharata* epic, 156 cm, parchment, ca. early 1930s. The puppeteers remarked that this particular puppet had special significance because of its age. It is remarkable for its fine carving, especially the incisions outlining the eyebrows and mustache and the way each individual finger is cut out. Its colors are less bright than puppets made later in the era of color movies, yet they achieve a striking effect with their deep richness.

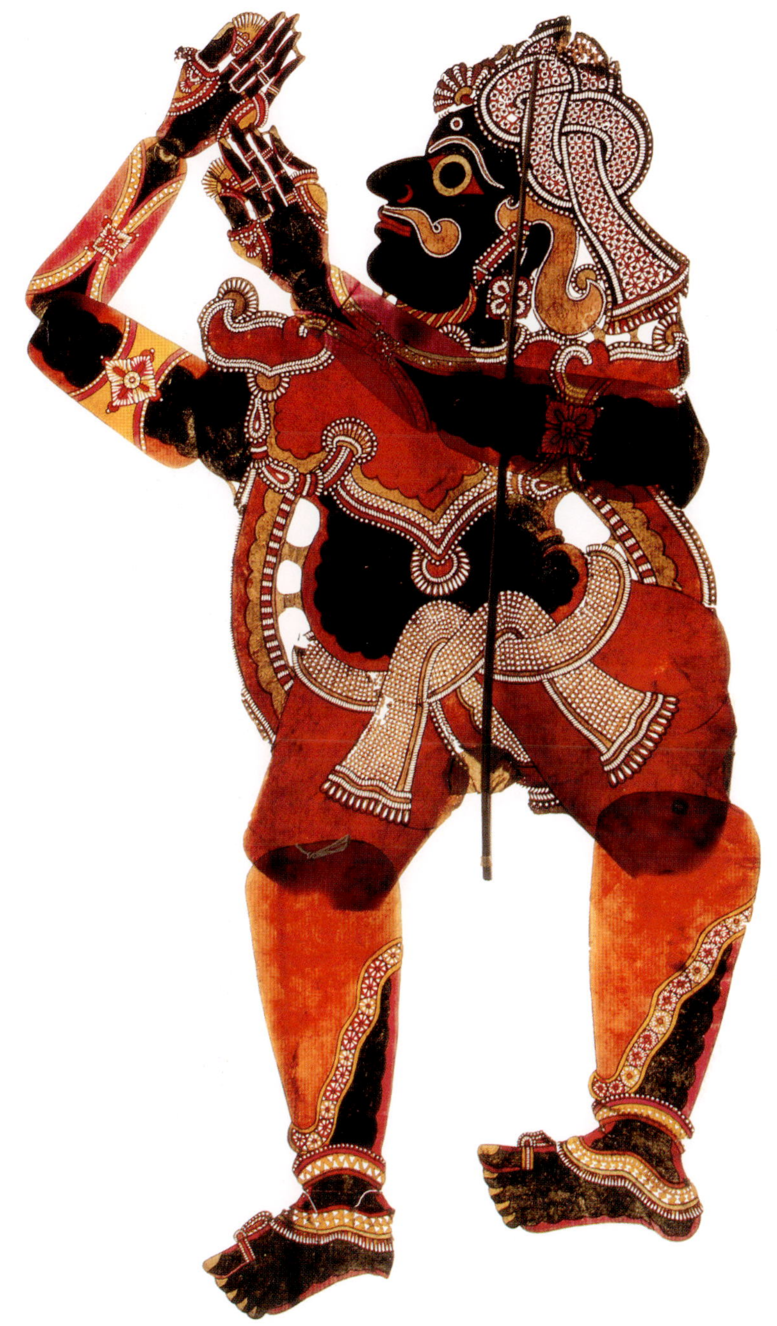

keeping her hips swaying to create a remarkable illusion of twirling.

The puppeteers accompanied all the characters' speeches with animated movement of arms and hands, which they flipped over to create a three-dimensional effect. The swaying of freely dangling legs also added to the feeling of animation. When several puppets were stationary on the screen at the same time, they were pinned to the screen with date palm thorns. A puppet would be rapidly pinned with one or two of the long, thin thorns passed through the perforations in its headdress or shoulder ornaments. Such puppets were still able to engage in animated conversation by

■ Ravana (Ravanudu), ten-headed evil king of Lanka who abducted Rama's wife Sita in the *Ramayana* epic, 176 cm, parchment, ca. 1950s. This puppet is one of the largest characters. He is depicted with ten arms, four being passively suspended from each main right and left arm. This puppet is the only one to represent a character's face frontally, apparently necessitated by depicting his other heads in profile. Presumably his tenth head is to the rear of the nine heads visible.

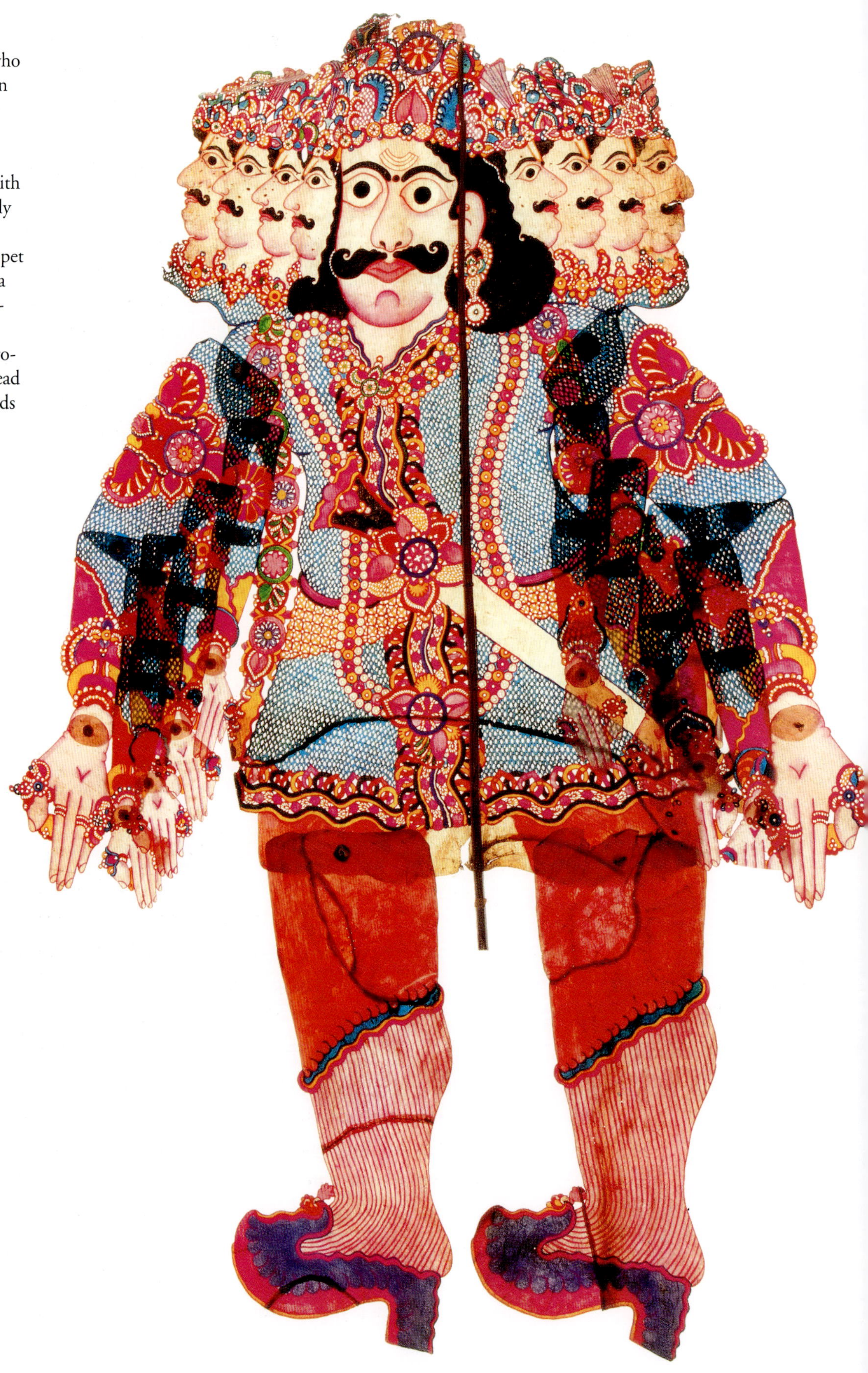

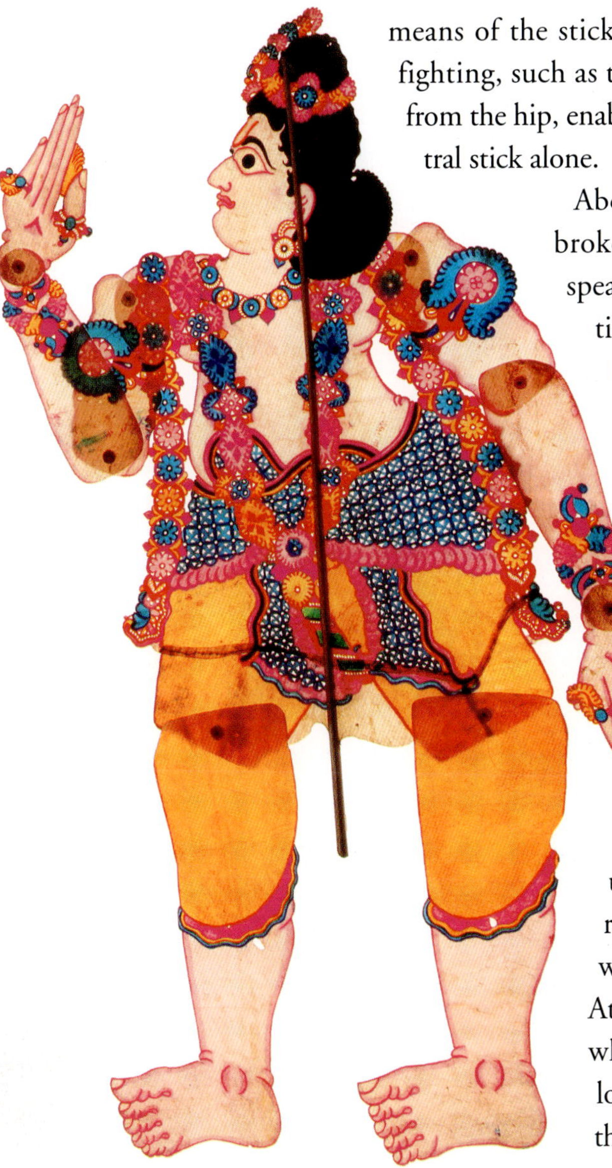

means of the sticks moving their hands. Characters that engaged in rough fighting, such as the monkey king Hanuman or the jesters, were often held from the hip, enabling them to be moved with greater control than by the central stick alone.

About five times throughout the performance the action was broken up by episodes of broad comic relief from the jesters, speaking in a slangy, quirky style and engaging in slapstick antics. Some of these depended on a strong dose of scatological humor or puns and risqué allusions to illicit sexual relations. Except for certain commonly used expletives, their language was not obscene, though sequences were bawdy to a degree not observed in other popular forms of entertainment. The gawky jester known as Allatappayya had a prominent penis that could be raised for comic effect by the puppeteers pulling a string. In one scene he mockingly mimicked intercourse with a slain demon's severed head, to the audience's great amusement.

During the performance, curious members of the audience often went to peer at the shadow players backstage. There one could see a sari rigged up in hammock fashion to hold puppets needed for the current scene but not on the screen at the moment. The players would periodically send out for glasses of tea and country rum. At times, late in the night, a member of the troupe would doze while one player and a musician could sustain a long monologue. A young boy was in charge of the fight scenes, slamming the puppets together while making loud banging noises against two boards with his foot in a wooden shoe.

■ Kusa, one of the twin sons of Rama, 111 cm, parchment, inscription dated 1958. With his hair in a topknot and his bare feet, he is depicted as a young boy or student.

Interspersed with the spoken dialogue, verse passages in literary Telugu and even Sanskrit were sung accompanied by music. These occurred especially in contexts of heightened emotion or important events, rather like arias in European operas. The players served as their own musicians, and all members of the troupe knew the music that accompanied the various passages.

The musical instruments consisted of a harmonium, a portable keyboard organ that sometimes served only as a drone; a long, two-headed South Indian drum with tapering ends (*mrdangam*); strings of bells worn on the ankles and wrists; and pairs of finger cymbals. A wooden shoe, a type with stilts used to keep its wearer above the mud during the rainy season, was struck against schoolchildren's seating planks to create dramatic clacking and banging sound effects for fight scenes.

The singing style and the conventions of vocal delivery for the play closely

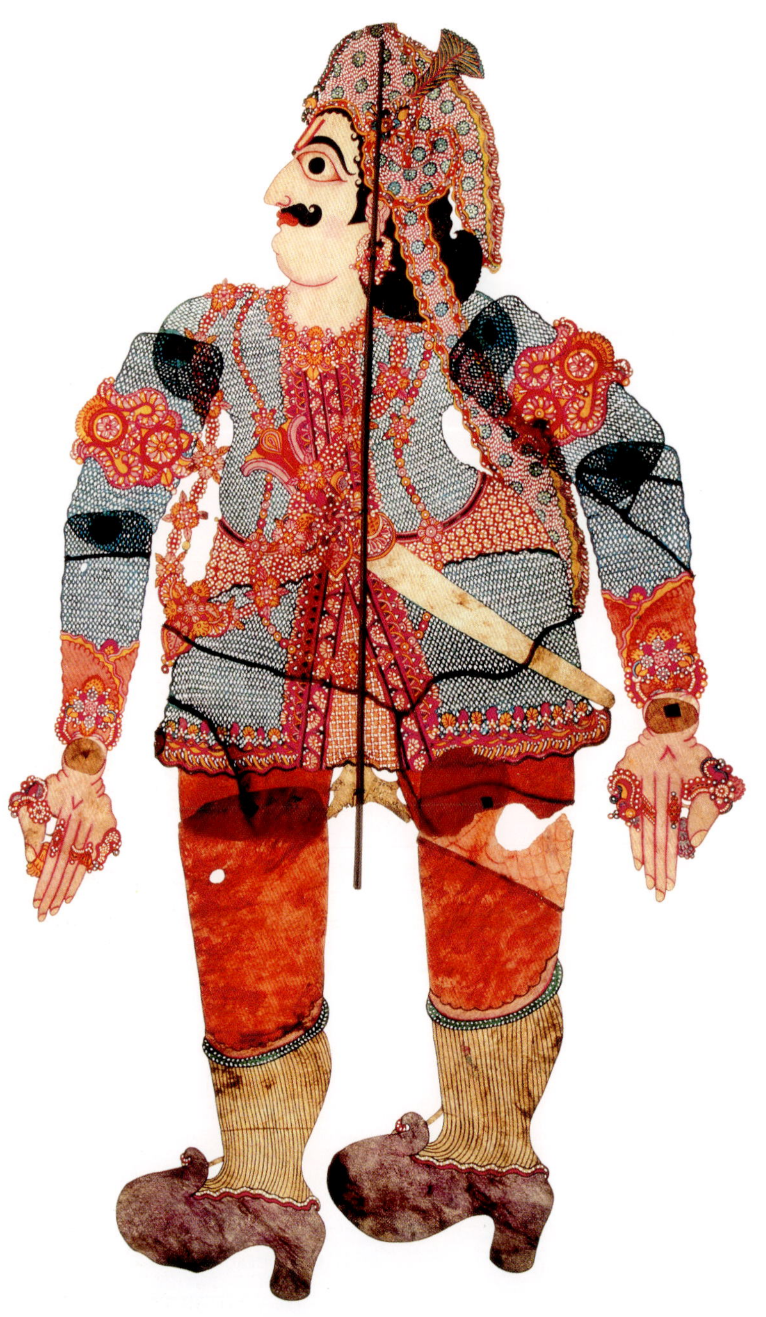

■ Karna (Karnudu), fighter for the Kauravas, 167.5 cm, parchment, inscription dated 1955. Among the noteworthy features of this figure are the filigreelike jacket covered with small holes and the colorful turban adorned with a jeweled ornament.

resembled the form of singing in an old-fashioned drama genre known as *Satyabhamakalapam.* Accompanied only by the drum and finger cymbals, the player sings, raising his hand up to one ear, almost as if to listen to what he is singing.

PUPPETS AND CINEMA

The whole performance had been a thrill for me, but apparently not for several villagers, who volubly complained after the show that this was a primitive form of

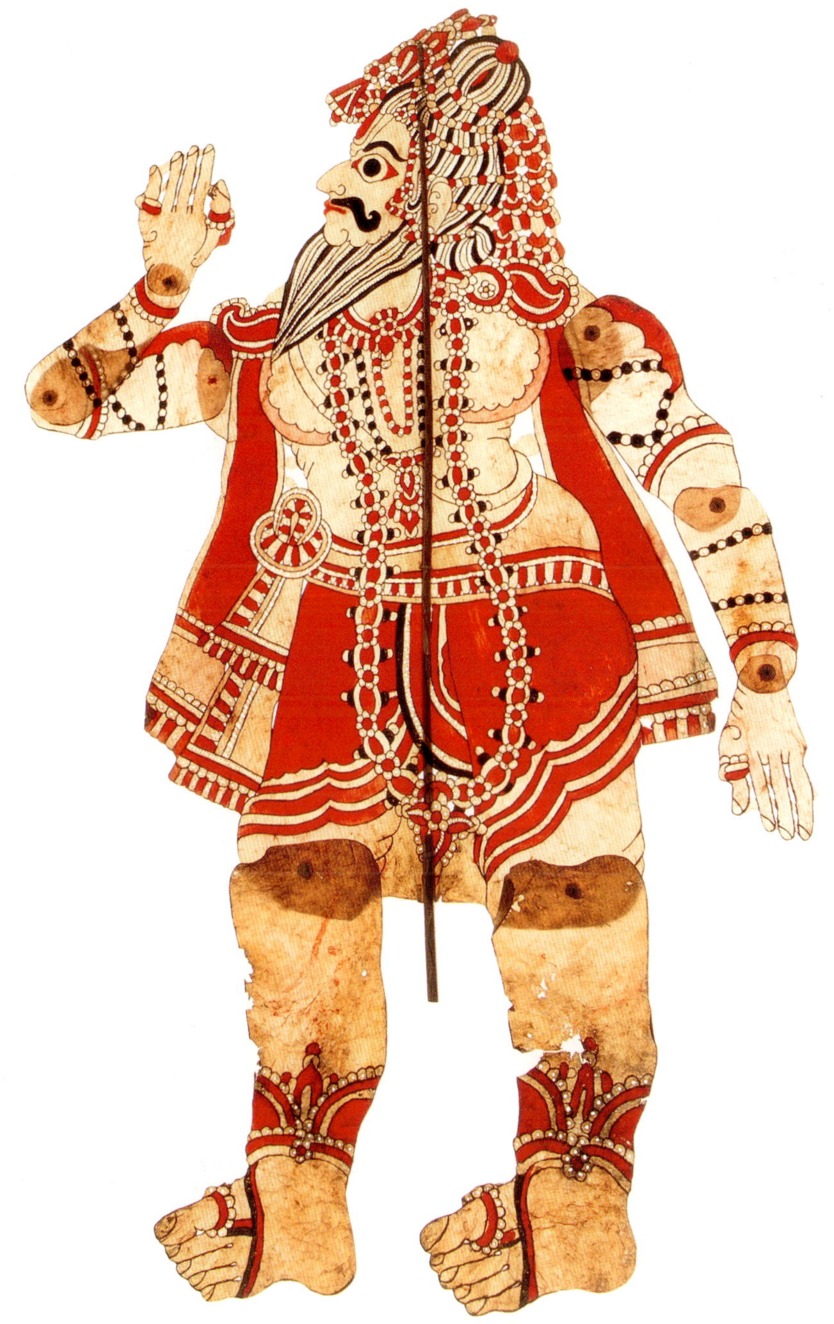

■ Drona (Dronacharya), sage in the *Mahabbharata* who was the preceptor of both the Pandavas and the Kauravas, 129 cm, parchment, ca. 1950s. The beard, topknot, and bare feet are characteristic of a holy man, here depicted in a limited range of colors.

drama unworthy of our attention and certainly undeserving of the fee I had agreed to pay them. "What do we need this for, when we have cinemas?" one villager remarked. In the face of this hostility, the troupe hastily departed, leaving many questions unanswered.

That the villagers compared shadow play to movies was informative. Shadow play was an ingenious technology of animating pictures, developed centuries before the advent of the motion picture industry. Here was a method of enabling four or five people to bring a hundred or more colorful mythological characters to life in the most remote village, all accompanied by virtuoso singing, contagious rhythms,

■ Sasirekha, daughter of Balarama in the *Mahabharata* epic, 95.5 cm, parchment, ca. 1940s. Major female characters are depicted wearing saris that conceal their legs. They are also considerably smaller in stature than the major male figures. This puppet seems stylistically older and more traditional than some of the other female characters by virtue of the limited range of colors, the method of wrapping the sari between the legs, the depiction of the hair in a bun, and the checked blouse. The sweep of the bottom of the sari echoes South Indian frescoes of the Vijayanagar period. Note how the puppet shows wear at the waist and around the bottom at the handle.

■ (Opposite, top) Sarama, wife of Vibhishana (brother of the evil king Ravana who defects to aid Rama) in the *Ramayana* epic, 101 cm, parchment, inscription at the base dated 1958. Her sari is in the style of a skirt with a separate shoulder piece. She has flowers in her hair.

■ (Opposite, bottom) Rajanarthaki, a dancing girl, 121 cm, parchment, mid-20th century. Note the jointed waist, lack of a central stick, and ornamental tassles and braids that enhance her movements when manipulated to music. Her head is a separate piece on a stick, secured through a loop of string to the body, that is swiveled to give the impression of twirling and intensify the rhythmic shifting of the shoulders.

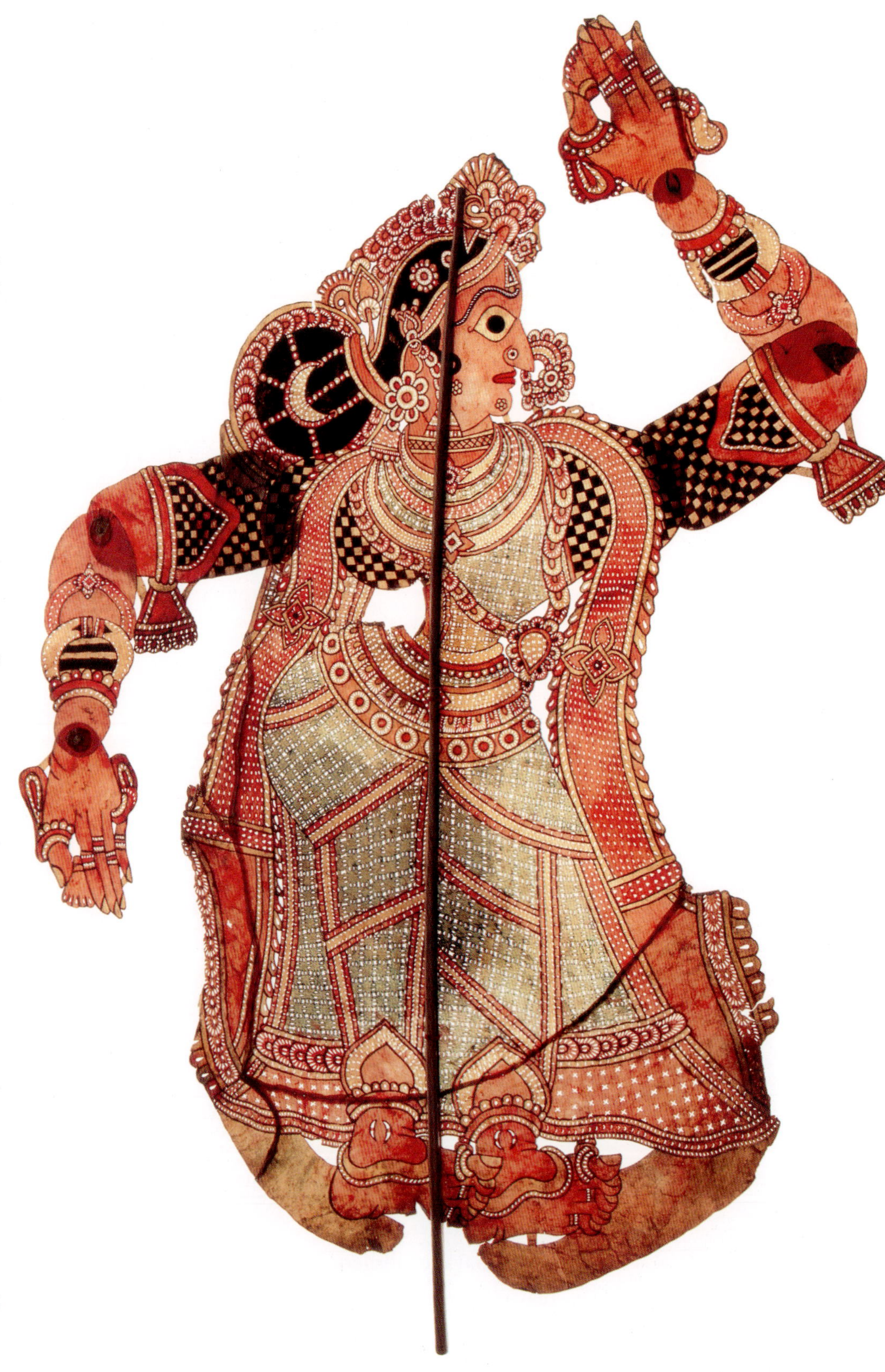

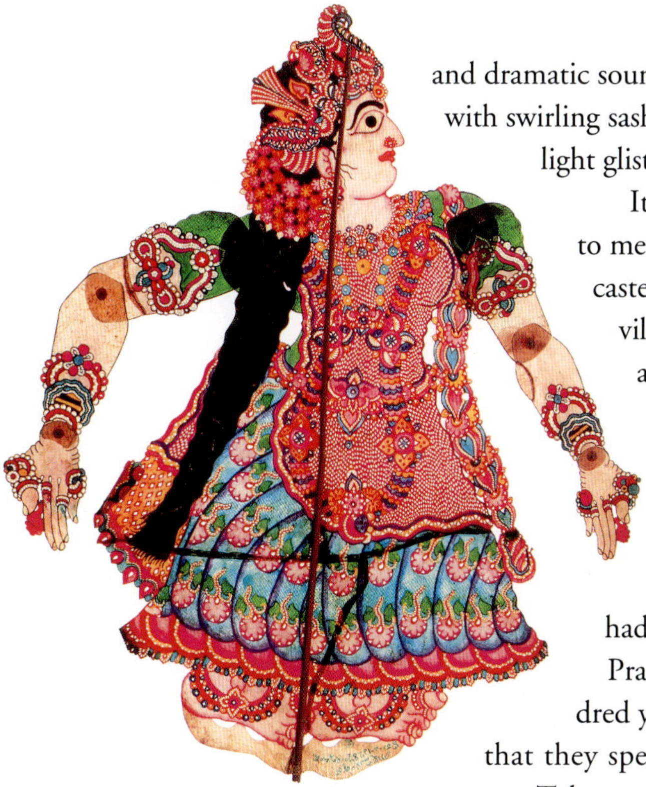

and dramatic sound effects. And how elaborate the characters' costumes were, with swirling sashes and ornate necklaces and garlands, all cut to let points of light glisten in intricate patterns.

It was another six months before I had another opportunity to meet shadow players. An itinerant troupe of the Telaga Bondili caste on its way through Subbavaram suggested I go to its home village in the East Godavari District, a five-hour railway journey away. This turned out to be a large village with many Telaga Bondili families. There I met with village elders and interviewed members of several shadow player families, obtaining puppets and shadow play manuscripts for further study.

The Telaga Bondili performers told me their ancestors had migrated to the Godavari delta from southwestern Andhra Pradesh, near the border with Karnataka, as much as two hundred years ago. Clues to the group's origins are hinted by the fact that they speak a language among themselves at home that is neither Telugu nor apparently a member of the Dravidian language family of South India. They called it Maharashtri but stressed that it was not the same as Marathi, the northern Indian language of the state of Maharashtra that lies north of Andhra and Karnataka.

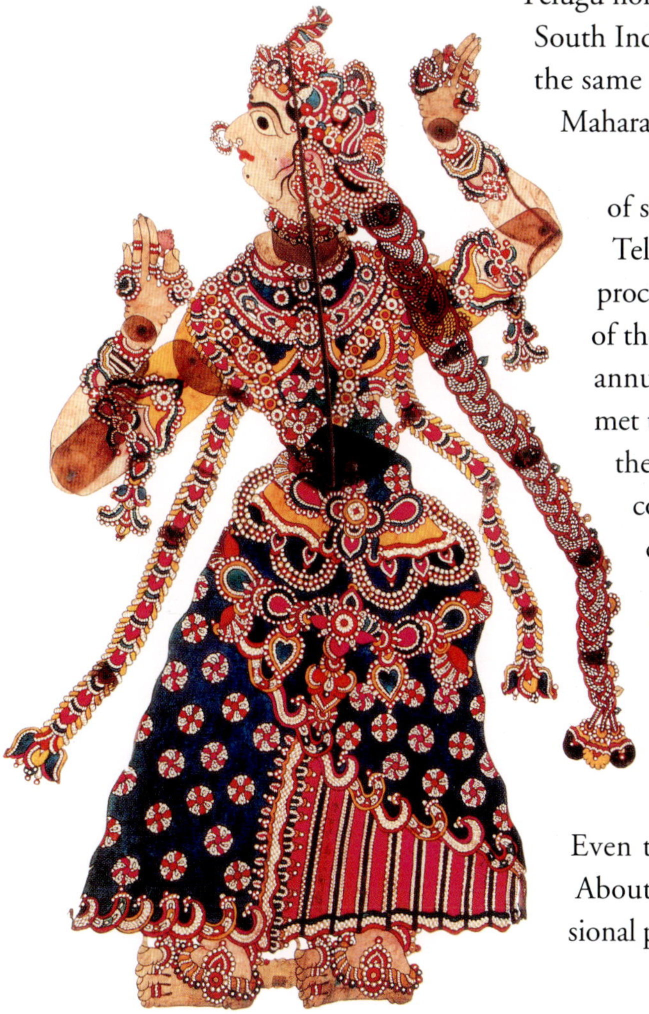

During my visit, the players confirmed that the popularity of shadow play had severely declined with the advent of the Telugu film industry. This state of affairs had been a gradual process. The Telugu cinema industry, based in Madras and one of the most vigorous in India, began in 1931.[1] The industry was annually producing seven feature films by 1948. By the time I met these performers, it was producing more than fifty. And by the early 1970s, all new films were being released in color. A considerable number of these films were lavish productions dealing specifically with mythological themes. With the spread of cinema halls accessible to rural areas, villagers had come to look upon the shadow play as a rude, rustic art not to be compared with the sophistication of the films.

As a consequence, only about a fifth of the families were still actively performing shadow plays in 1972—some in remote tribal areas of Srikakulam District. Even those had to supplement their income by other means. About half of the families were hiring themselves out for occasional performances of ballad singing or dance dramas in the styles known as Harikatha, Burrakatha, and Bhamakalapam that have nothing to do with shadow plays. These utilized their skills in reciting poems, singing, and playing music but also threw them into competition with many other groups of performers. Another third of the families were fortunate enough to have acquired agricultural lands for farming. This had been accomplished partly with money earned by relatives migrating to work for cash in Burma—a source of opportunity disrupted by the

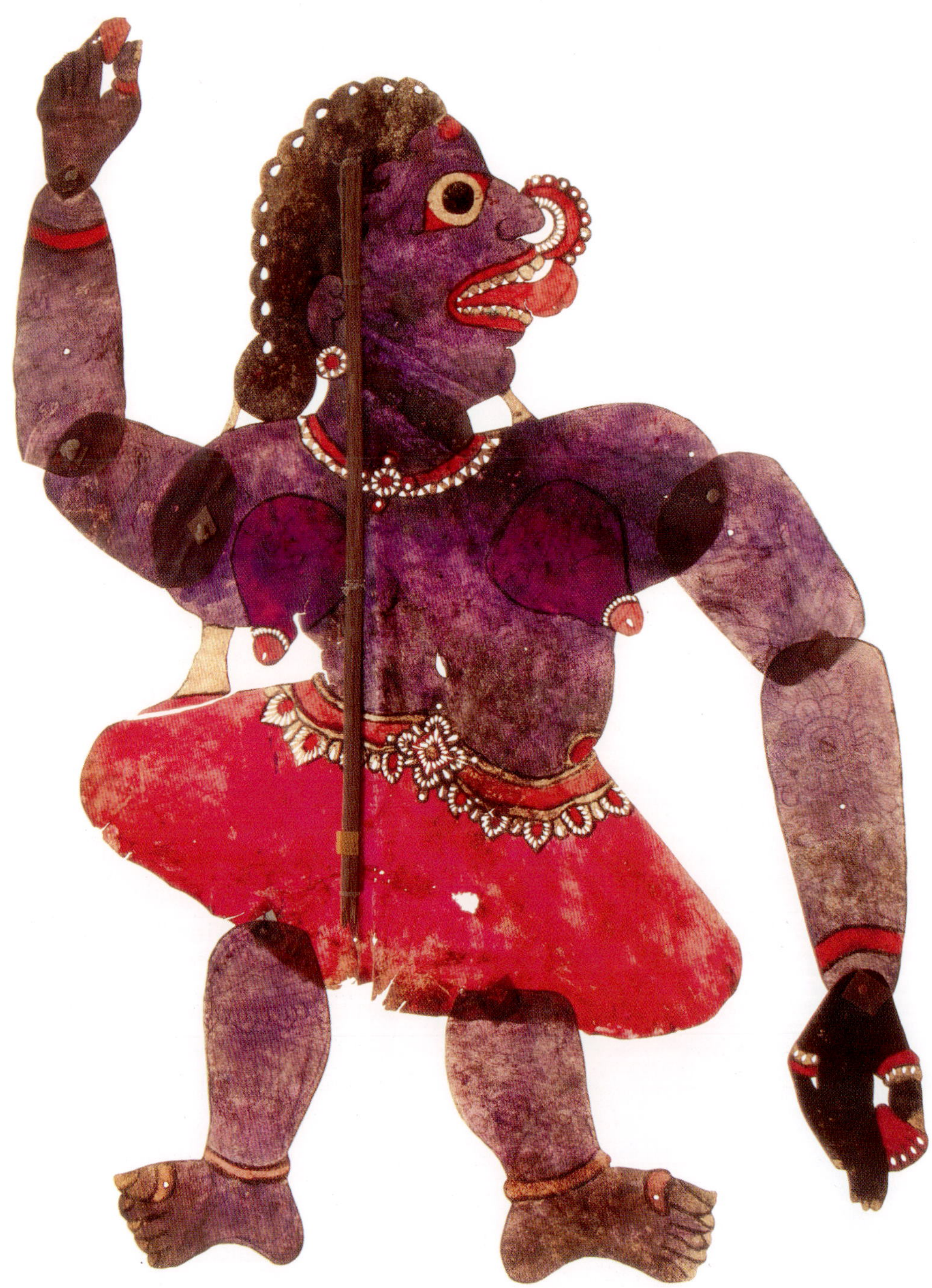

■ Bangarakka, the jester wife of Allatappayya, 66 cm, parchment, mid-20th century. She has gross features, including bare breasts, exposed legs, and lolling tongue.

■ (Opposite, bottom) Allatappayya, 102 cm, parchment, ca. mid-1950s. Goat hair is used for underarm and pubic hair as well as for his head and chin. His gawky neck and irregular nose are reflected in the quirky voice often associated with this jester character. This puppet has been damaged and partly repaired, with a hand lacking the usual dagger. The pubic hair suggests that the puppet probably once had a prominent phallus.

■ (Right) Allatappayya, 70 cm, parchment, mid-20th century. There are actual tufts of goat hair on his head and chin. His phallus is raised for bawdily humorous effect by pulling a string. These attributes signal his cruder character, which leaves him free to amuse the audience with slangy speech and slapstick antics during comic intervals from the main drama. His social stature is also mirrored by his height; he is shorter than the major male characters.

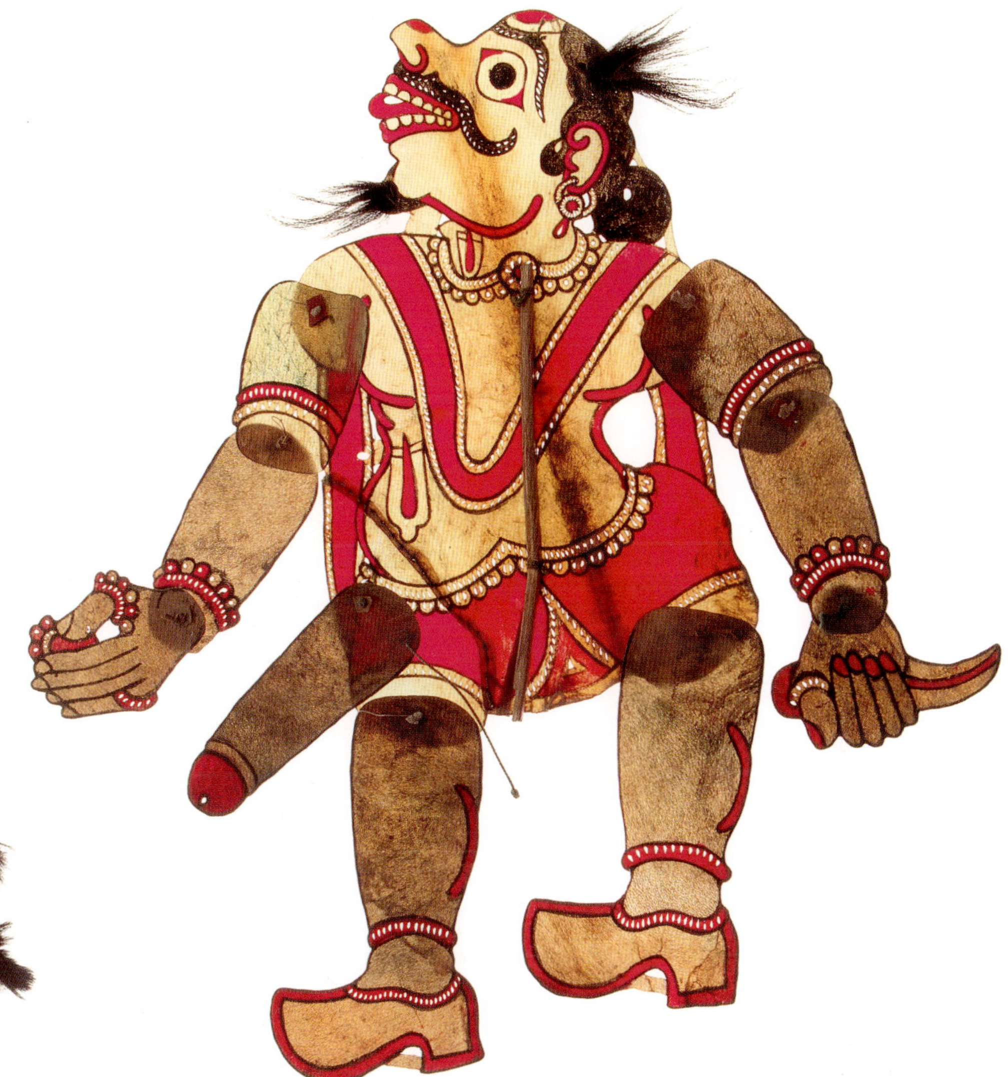

Second World War and finally ended after Burmese independence, when most Indians were forced out.

The Telaga Bondili people said that one of the most important sources of their income had now become trade in old clothes and aluminum cooking pots. In towns they would trade new pots for old clothes, which they repaired and sold in rural areas. This pattern of circulating among villages repeated their traditional custom of wandering, but it seemed pathetic that the heirs of such a unique traditional art form were reduced to this.

A sorry expression of the plight of these families was their account of how they abandoned their shadow puppets because they could no longer earn a living from them. They described taking the puppets out on the Godavari River or to the Bay of Bengal and respectfully submerging them in the water, taking their leave of the puppet characters in the same way Hindus traditionally send off the clay image of a deity at the end of a festival.

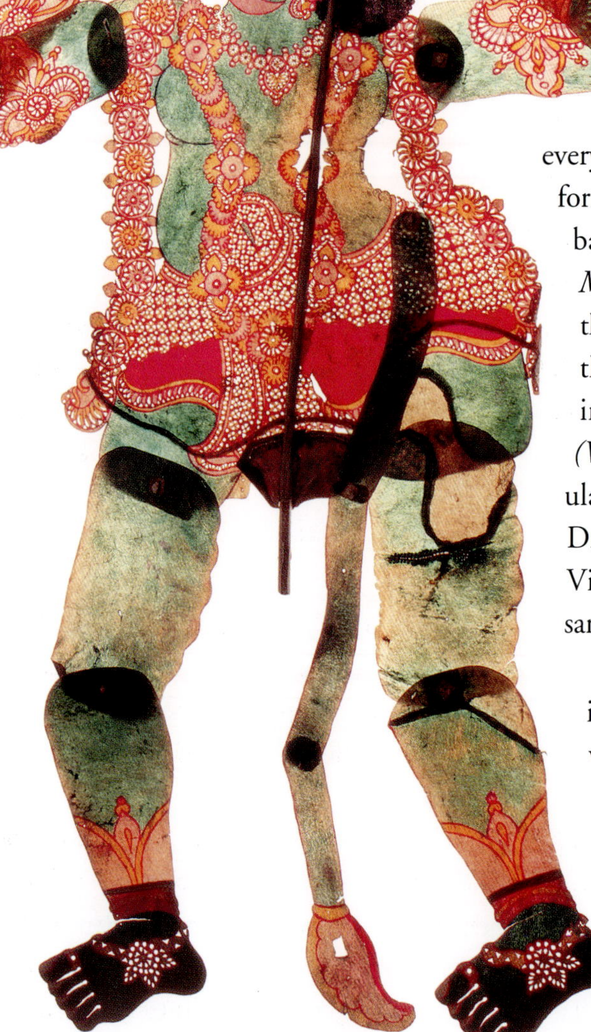

■ Hanuman (Hanumanta), monkey king who aids Rama in the *Ramayana* epic, 132 cm, parchment, ca. mid-1950s. Monkey warriors are usually jointed at the knees, unlike the major male characters, and have a jointed tail. The wear around the central stick on his chest is due to use in fighting scenes.

CHARACTERS AND STORIES

The shadow players reported that, traditionally, every family troupe had two sets of shadow puppets to perform a repertoire of about eight of the most popular plays based on episodes in the two major Hindu epics, the *Mahabharata* and the *Ramayana.* In the entire village there was only one set of puppets for plays not relating to these two major epics. Four of the *Mahabharata* plays in the repertoire are based on the Book of Virata *(Virataparvam),* describing the year in which the popular Pandava heroes (five brothers and their wife Draupadi) assumed disguises and lived incognito in King Virata's court—the result of a wager lost to their adversaries, the Kauravas.

In one of the plays, *Kichakavadha,* Virata's minister of war, Kichaka, makes advances toward Draupadi, who is disguised as a maidservant. Bhima, the Pandava renowned for his prodigious strength and here disguised as a cook, has her lure Kichaka to a night rendezvous and then kills him and all his brothers in a furious battle. But nobody knows the true identity of the slayer. The story is picked up in a second play, *Uttaragograhanam.* Spies of the Kaurava Duryodhana, seeking the whereabouts of the Pandavas, hear of the surprising killing of Kichaka. The evidence leads to suspicion of Bhima. Duryodhana and an ally plot to lure the Pandavas out of hiding by stealing the herds of King Virata's cattle. The king's son takes the advice of Draupadi, still disguised as a maidservant, and enlists as his charioteer a transvestite dancing instructor in the court, Bruhannala, who happens to be noble Arjuna, the Pandava, in disguise. When Virata's son lacks courage in the face of Duryodhana's forces, Arjuna has him take down the miraculous weapons of the Pandavas, which have been hidden in a tree. Arjuna blows his thunderous conch, and they go off to battle. Since the Pandavas' year of hiding is completed, they can come out into the open and freely fight and recapture King Virata's cows.

The following excerpt is from a Telaga Bondili manuscript text of *Uttaragograhanam,* at the point at which Duryodhana is trying to figure out where the Pandavas might be hiding. It offers a glimpse of the kind of traditional moral precepts conveyed by the shadow play. In the scene, Bhishma (a family elder related to both Kauravas and Pandavas) tells Duryodhana:

> [Prose] I do not know where the Pandavas are now living, but I can tell you that wherever it may be, the people of that town or village or country will be like this—
>
> [Verse] They will have respect for Brahmans. They will be benevolent and of pure mind. They will obey sexual morality and will speak the truth. They will nurture sages and holy men. They will be worshipful. They will protect the virtuous and punish the stupid. They will show kindness to their relatives. They will live according to the precepts of the *Shastras.* The people in a place where the Pandavas are living will be righteous and have abundant wealth and rice.

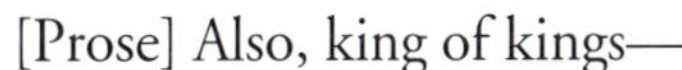

> [Prose] Also, king of kings—
>
> [Verse] I shall disclose one more quality. In a country in which the Pandavas live there will be a great many cows, and the people will never be short of dairy foods. The cows will yield milk like a shower of rain.

At this point the spies tell Duryodhana that the Matsya Kingdom ruled by King Virata fits this description.

An inventory of one particular family's *Mahabharata* puppets revealed 86 characters, 13 animals, and 4 props, constituting a total of 103 puppets, excluding invocatory deities, dancing girls, and jesters. Its *Ramayana* set consisted of 64 characters, 14 animals, and 23 props, for a total of 101 items.

The performers stored and transported the puppets in a flat rectangular basket. The large male puppet characters are constructed so that their arms and legs can fold up over their bodies to enable them to fit into the much smaller dimensions of the basket. There is no prescribed order for placing most of the puppets, but it is considered essential to place the puppet of the female jester, Bangarakka, on the top of the pile. Her placement is related to her function of absorbing

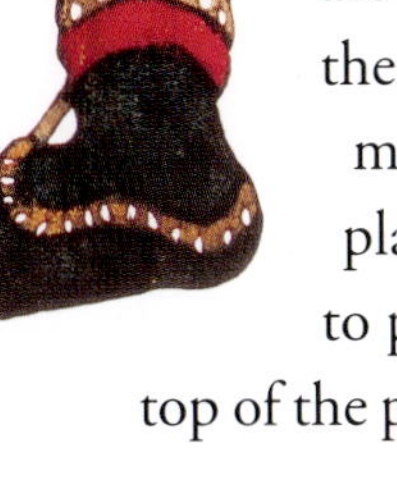

■ Tiny Hanuman, of the kind when he sits in the tree under which Sita is being held in captivity in Lanka, 54 cm (from top of head to bottom of hanging arm; 30.5 cm horizontally from tip of nose to rump), parchment, mid-1950s. This puppet's arms are not manipulated by the puppeteers, who instead move the entire figure to show it flying through the air or perched on a branch.

■ Lankini, a demoness who guards the approaches to the island of Lanka, 146 cm (with detachable head, 54 cm, in place), parchment, mid-20th century. This puppet's detachable head enables her to be beheaded in battle in the *Ramayana* epic. In addition to the gross nature of her face—daggerlike teeth and prominent tongue protruding from her open mouth—she is immodestly bare breasted and has legs exposed from under her skirt. In some respects she shares these traits with the female jester, Bangarakka, but is far larger and more menacing. Note the structural supports in the construction of the puppet's nose, hair bun, and fingertips.

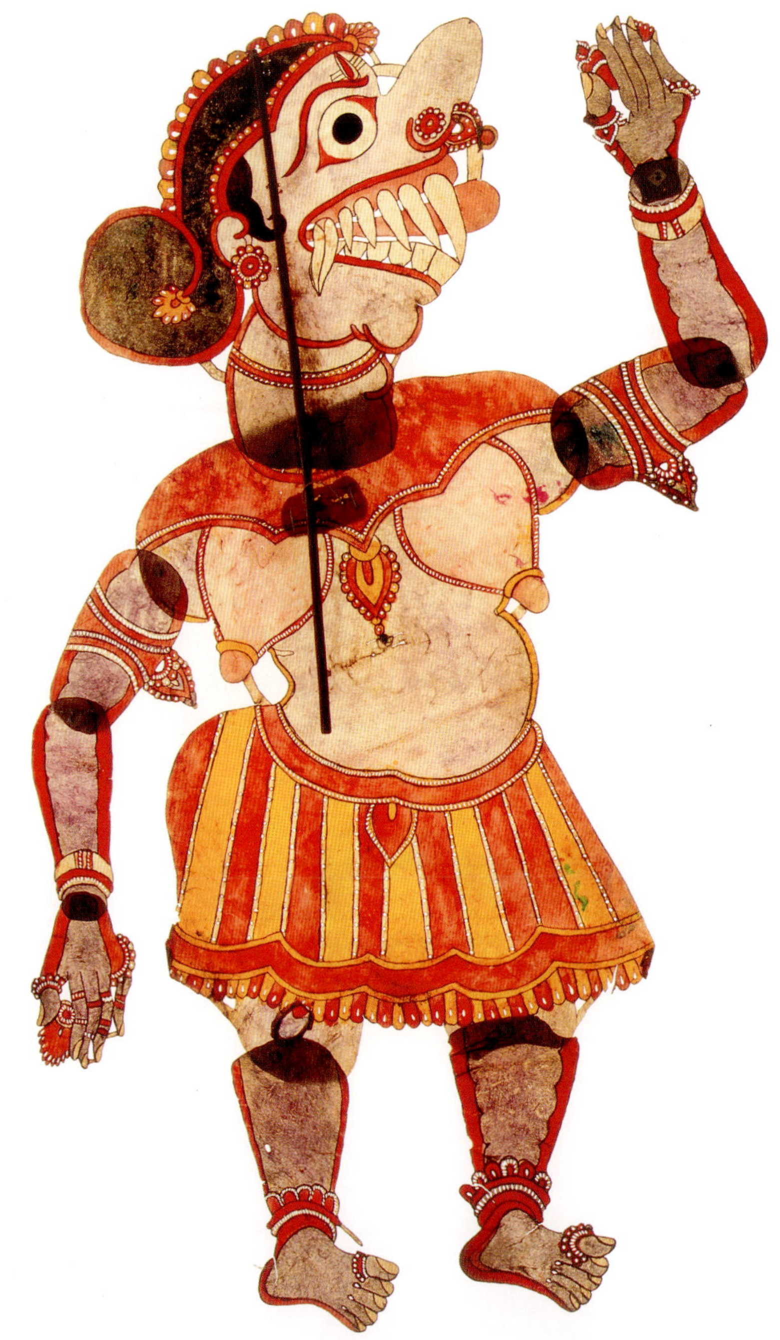

and counteracting the evil eye. In addition, the chief heroines, Sita and Draupadi, are never placed next to the puppets of their would-be ravishers, Ravana and Duryodhana, respectively. Like idols in Hindu temples, the puppets in some respects are the characters they represent.

While the variety of shadow puppets is large, the number of puppets identifiable as particular characters is much smaller. In fact, a great many puppets are used to represent different characters in the various plays. Princes and courtiers tend to look the same, as do many puppets of women. For the more important charac-

■ Rakshasa (Rakshasudu), a type of demon from the *Ramayana* epic, 130 cm, parchment, mid-20th century. Henchmen of the evil king Ravana frequently appear in groups with their prominent ghoulish faces. This puppet appears actually to have attacked its maker, causing him to fall ill, as evidenced by the exorcistic holes in its teeth. In Hindu belief, images can become the character they depict, hence the potential danger from a puppet representing a demon. Following the same logic, puppeteers take care to avoid storing puppets of antagonistic characters directly in contact with each other.

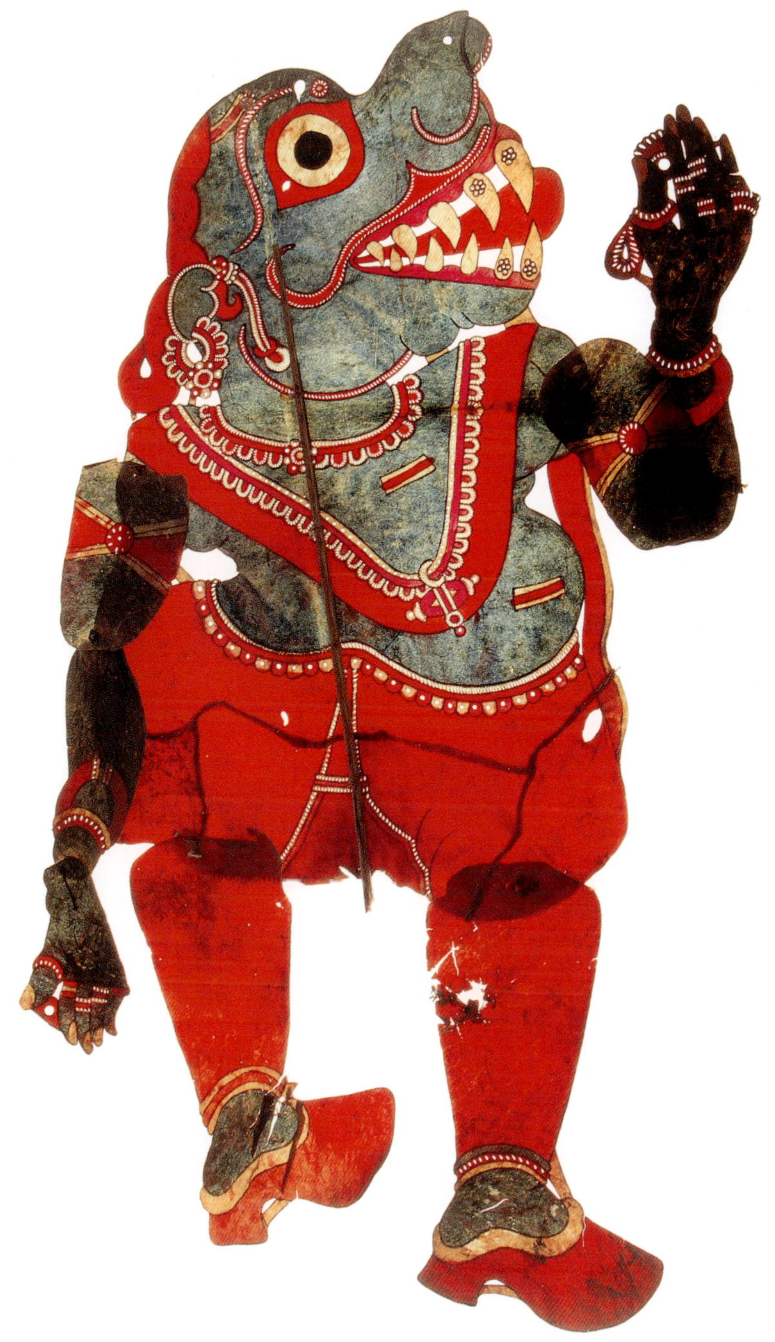

ters—such as Rama, Hanuman, Arjuna, and Bhima—there is an elaboration in the opposite direction, with multiple figures representing them in different disguises or stages in their careers.

Other general distinctions in the characters cluster around sex and category—main characters, sages, demons, and jesters. Most male characters range between 150 and 175 centimeters in height, while females are 90–100 centimeters. Both sexes have jointed arms, but only males have freely hanging legs. Women's legs are concealed beneath their saris, and only their feet are visible. Some deities are depicted with blue skin; the monkey Hanuman is sometimes dark green or black. Sages have beards and topknots. Demons are generally large, with disproportionately big heads and noses. They also have large open mouths, lolling tongues, and rows of pointed teeth. Female demons are bare breasted and wear short skirts that immodestly expose their legs. Jesters are small, between 75 and 100 centimeters in height including their freely dangling legs. The male jesters have beards or goatees, and tufts of actual goat hair are often attached to the character of Allatappayya. Their mouths are open with tongue and teeth showing. They often have exaggerated Adam's apples and may hold a dagger. Male jesters often have prominent exposed penises.

Certain items of clothing conventionally depicted on puppets appear to hark back to earlier periods. Among these are the decorated jacket with waist sash, worn over trousers or striped leggings. In the Telaga Bondili puppets, these leggings are now generally combined with representations of dhotis. Early sixteenth-century Vijayanagar paintings from Lepakshi in South India depict men with thigh-length jackets and elaborate waist sashes. They also show a bare-chested male fashion, encountered in puppets, with striped or patterned dhotis covered by a wide waist-cloth, in addition to women's checked saris and hairdos.[2] The most striking stylistic parallels of the Andhra shadow puppets are found in the so-called Paithan paintings. These are believed to have been used by wandering storytellers in nineteenth-century Maharashtra.

■ Makhari, crocodilelike sea monster in the *Ramayana* epic, 202.5 cm, parchment, mid-1950s. This puppet has control sticks in both jaws, with the lower one hinged to open to swallow adversaries.

Inscriptions that often appear at the base of a puppet figure record the maker and sometimes the name of a deceased family member and the exact date and place of his death. Puppets are often, though not exclusively, made in honor of a relative

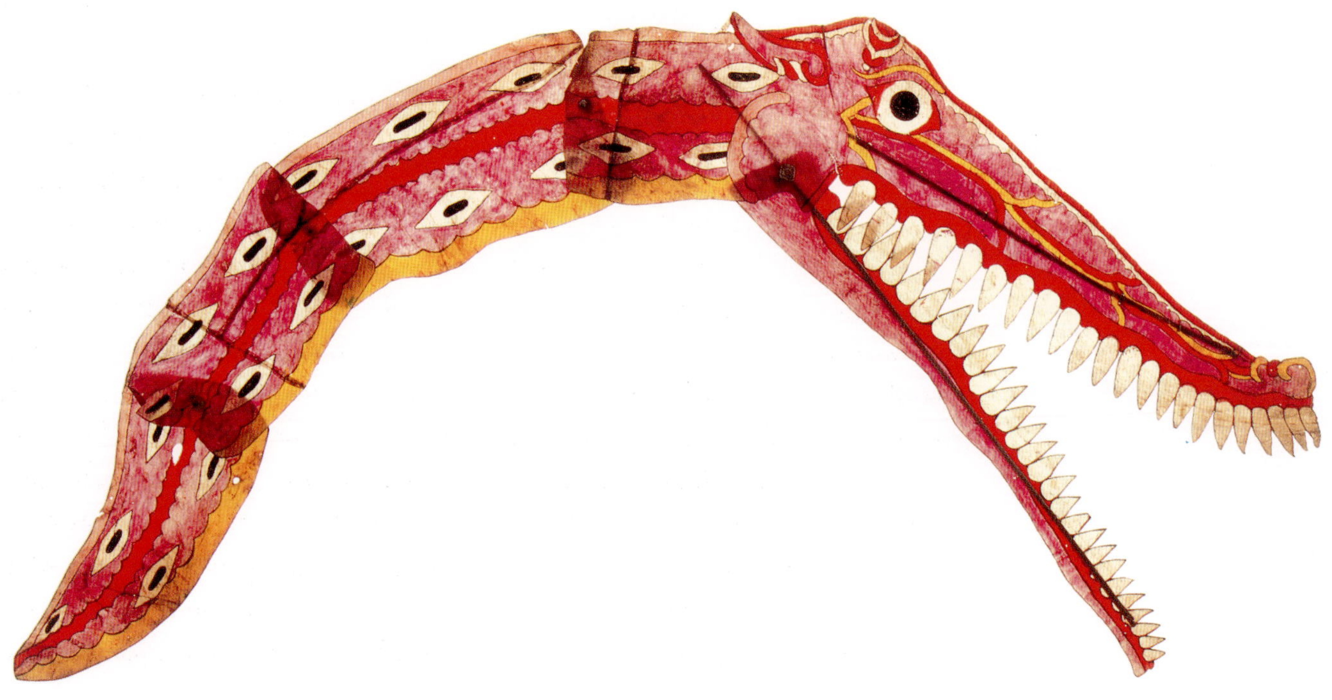

who has just died. The puppets are thus a direct link between puppeteers and their deceased elders.

The high-heeled shoes depicted on male puppets also offer stylistic information. Some have a sort of turned-up toe with a bell or tuft at the end, while others have a flatter toe. Many have no backs. It seems possible that these shoes are related to types of traditional shoes worn in western Maharashtra in which the back is folded down, so they resemble slippers. Some varieties of shoes are more elaborate and perhaps the product of the puppeteers' imaginations. In any case, it is significant that, south of Maharashtra, traditional peoples did not wear shoes.[3]

PUPPET MAKING

The puppeteers explained they use three types of skins to manufacture puppets—antelope, spotted deer, and goat. Antelope skins, obtained from tribal peoples in the far northeast of Andhra Pradesh, are reserved for making a limited number of auspicious characters such as the gods and epic heroes. Deerskin, noted for its strength and resistance to rough handling, is employed in the figures of the warrior, Bhima; the ten-headed demon king, Ravana; and the wrestlers Jimutamallu and Jirghavudu. All other puppets are made from goatskin, readily available locally. Most puppets are made from a single skin, though some require more. At least four skins are necessary for Ravana—one for his body, one for his legs, and one to make each set of five arms.

The puppeteers described soaking the skins in hot water until the fur loosens. They scrape the fur off and dry the skin, repeating the process up to fifteen times to achieve the desired degree of translucence. Strictly speaking, the puppets are made of parchment and not leather, since no tanning process is involved.

Once the skin is prepared, the puppeteers scratch on an outline of a new puppet. Constantly going over the outline with a graverlike instrument makes superfluous pieces fall away. Then they apply the main areas of color with brushes purchased commercially. Pieces of iron of varying widths are used to draw finer lines. Then comes the elaboration of perforations. The puppeteers employ nearly twenty tools for cutting holes, some of which have special names. Except for circular holes made with a punch, each perforation is individually constructed by hand. The principal shapes are triangles, semicircles, hourglasslike figures of inverted triangles, crosses, plus teardrop- and rice grain-shaped slits. These are often arranged in rows, sometimes themselves forming checked or diamond patterns. On the whole, the perforations in the design are dictated by the drawn pattern rather than the reverse.

Today the pigments used are blue, red, and yellow dye powders purchased in towns and probably related to the colors sold throughout northern India for the festival of Holi. The puppeteers boil the dye powder, tree gum, and a plant root in an acid solution for an entire day. Black is obtained from pot soot collected by burning an oil lamp under a potsherd. The soot is boiled with another type of tree gum in a similar acid solution. The puppeteers could not supply information about the older techniques of dye making, but they said some families still had blocks of pigment handed down from previous generations. They said they preferred not to use the old colors because they were not as bright as the commercial colors.

The puppeteers reported that a completed puppet can "wink its eye," an event that can only be seen by the maker of the puppet and not anyone else present at the time. Such a puppet is believed to have attacked its owner, who then falls ill. One remedy is to punch one or a series of holes in the puppet—on its teeth, stomach, or leg. Such "attacks" are often associated with puppets that deviate from traditional designs—puppets that copy a temple sculpture or a calendar picture, for example. The frequency of actual cases would not need to be high for this belief to have served as a persuasive sanction, preserving styles over long periods of time.

A puppet is considered the property of a joint family as a whole and not the personal property of its maker. Children's shares in their families' puppets are weighted in favor of sons. In a family with a son and daughter, the puppeteers said the son would receive two quarter shares, the daughter one quarter, and the parents one quarter. A woman's share in her family's collection is given as her dowry at her wedding. Even after setting up separate households, sons are expected to give their

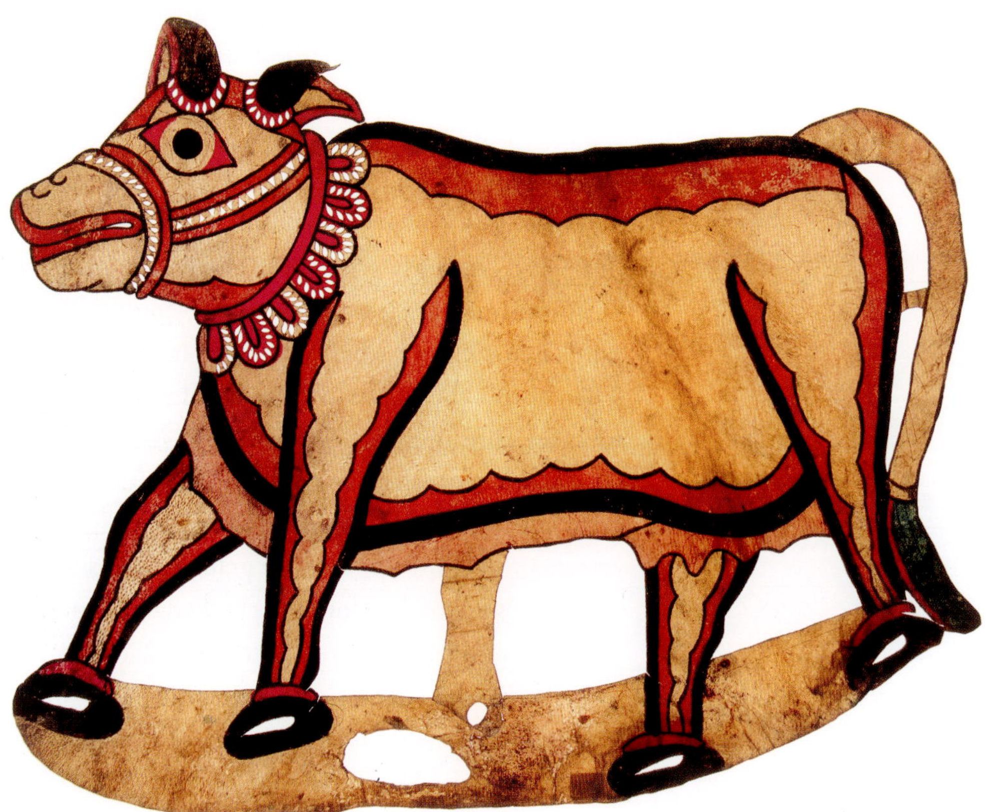

■ Cow featured in the cattle-rustling episode of the "Virataparvam" section of the *Mahabharata* epic, 40 cm (ear to hoof; 50.5 cm nose to tail), parchment, mid-20th century. The strip under the cow serves as a structural support.

■ Ashoka tree (Ashokavrksham) under which Sita sits in captivity in Lanka in the *Ramayana* epic, 102.5 cm (stick protrudes an additional 8 cm below), parchment, mid-20th century. The animals depicted appear to represent the sympathy of auspicious creatures sitting vigil with Sita and attest to her faithfulness to her husband, Rama. The five-headed cobra is often associated with the power of self-mastery of holy men doing religious penance. The large bird in the center is the Hamsa, a mythical swanlike creature. The chipmunk is a reference to a legend. When tiny chipmunks did their small part to build the causeway for Rama's forces by sprinkling dirt with their tails, Rama lovingly stroked one in appreciation. That is how the chipmunk got its stripes.

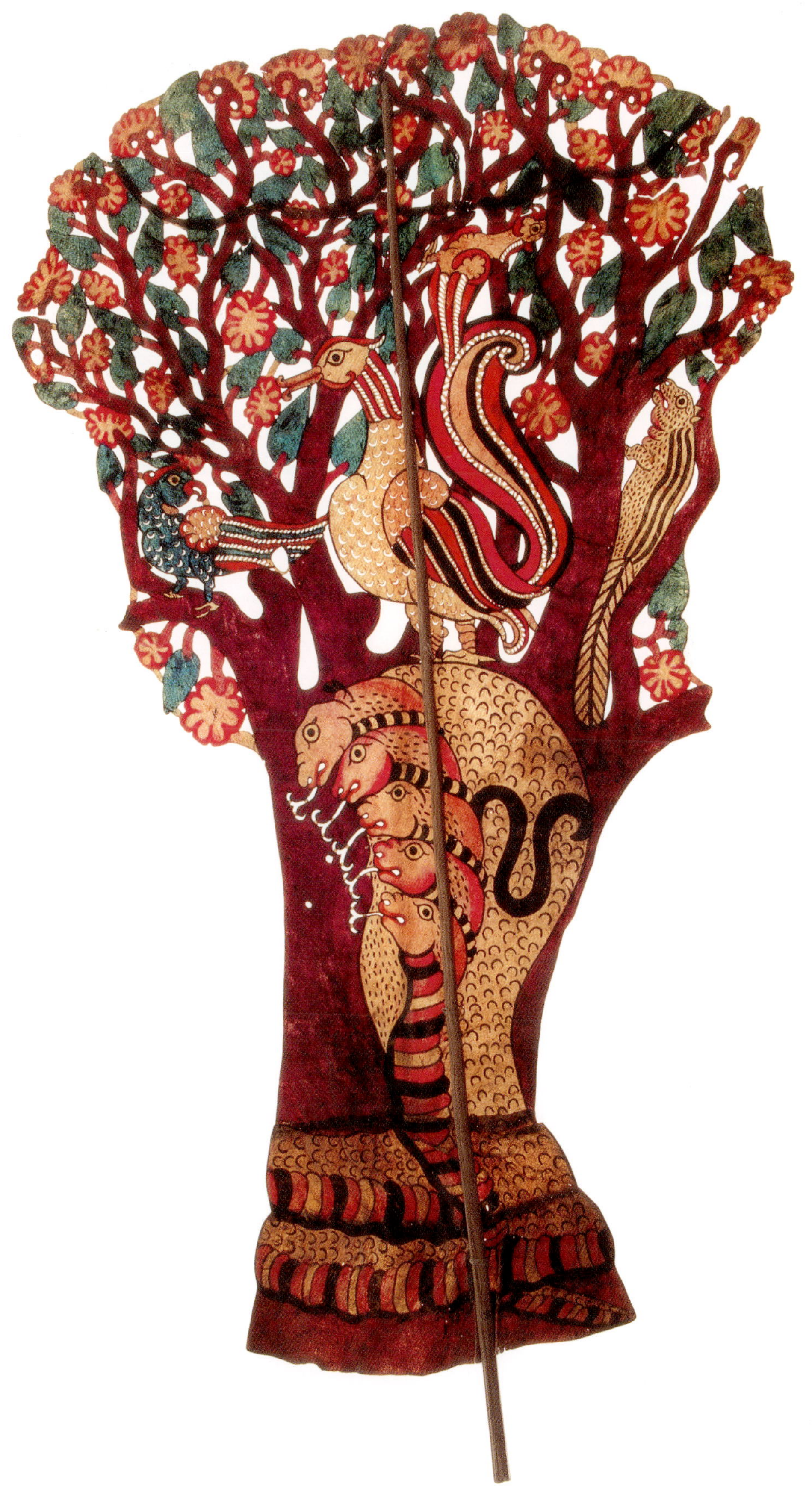

parents a share of money they receive for performing.

The puppeteers said that the festivals of Sri Rama Navami and Dasara were times when shadow play artists were traditionally in greatest demand. These are festivals lasting several days, during which people sponsor all sorts of entertainment. Sri Rama Navami is the celebration of the marriage of Rama and Sita, while Dasara is generally associated with the victory of Rama over Ravana. Though the puppeteers' Rama-related plays would have been appropriate they were never a requirement for any particular festival. This absence of a specific tie between shadow play and a festival, temple, or princely patron is probably an additional reason for the decline of this unique medium.

Shadow play was but one incarnation—one set of techniques for dramatizing the vastly rich Hindu epics. It is now superseded by motion pictures and television, which have reinvigorated the epics for the electronic age. But shadow play was a brilliant incarnation, one whose visual artifacts hold clues to the history of South Asian art and drama and deserve to be preserved for the delight of generations to come. ■

NOTES

1. Erik Barnouw and Subrahmanyam Krishnaswamy, *Indian Film* (New York: Columbia University Press, 1963), pp. 64, 100–115.

2. George Michell and Vasundhara Filliozat, *Splendours of the Vijayanagara Empire—Hampi* (Bombay: Marg Publications, 1981), pls. 10, 11; Amancharla Gopala Rao, *Lepakshi* (Hyderabad: Andhra Pradesh Lalit Kala Akademi, 1969), pl. III.

3. S. G. Morab, "Foot-Gear," in *Peasant Life in India: A Study in Indian Unity and Diversity,* ed. N. K. Bose, Anthropological Survey of India Memoir 8 (Calcutta: Anthropological Survey of India, 1961), pp. 49–54.

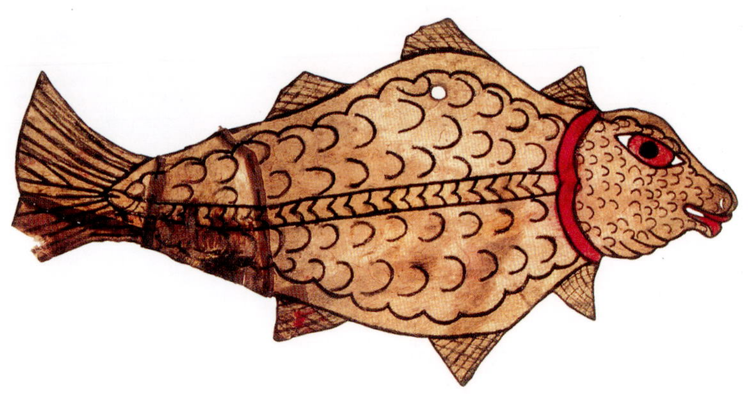

■ Fish, 47.5 cm (tip of tail to mouth), parchment, mid-20th century. This puppet is made from three pieces of parchment stitched together, perhaps scraps left over from the manufacture of larger characters.

FURTHER READING

Contractor, Meher. "Shadow Puppets." *Marg: A Magazine of the Arts* 21, no. 3 (1968): 20–38.

A short collection of articles by Contractor and K. B. Iyer that briefly describes shadow play traditions in several regions of India, including Andhra Pradesh, Tamil Nadu, Kerala, Karnataka, and Orissa.

Robbins, Kenneth X. "Indo-Asian Shadow Figures." *Arts of Asia,* 13 no. 5 (1983): 64–75.

Brief, illustrated summary of shadow play traditions in South and Southeast Asia.

Sekhar, A. Chandra, ed. "Leather Puppet Dolls." In *Selected Crafts of Andhra Pradesh* Part 7-A(1) 15–35, Census of India 1961, vol. 2, Andhra Pradesh, Manager of Publications, Delhi (1964).

Description of some Andhra shadow puppet manufacturing techniques, with additional information on performances.

UCLA Museum of Cultural History. *Asian Puppets: Wall of the World.* Los Angeles: UCLA Museum of Cultural History, 1976.

Exhibition catalogue that offers readers illustrations of shadow puppets from a number of Asian countries, including India.

■ Bruce Elliot Tapper earned a master's degree in South Asian studies at the University of Wisconsin, Madison, before obtaining his Ph.D. in social anthropology from the School of Oriental and African Studies, University of London. Currently a resident of the Washington, D.C., area, he is the author of *Rivalry and Tribute: Society and Ritual in a Telugu Village in South India* (Delhi: Hindustan Publishing Corp., 1987).

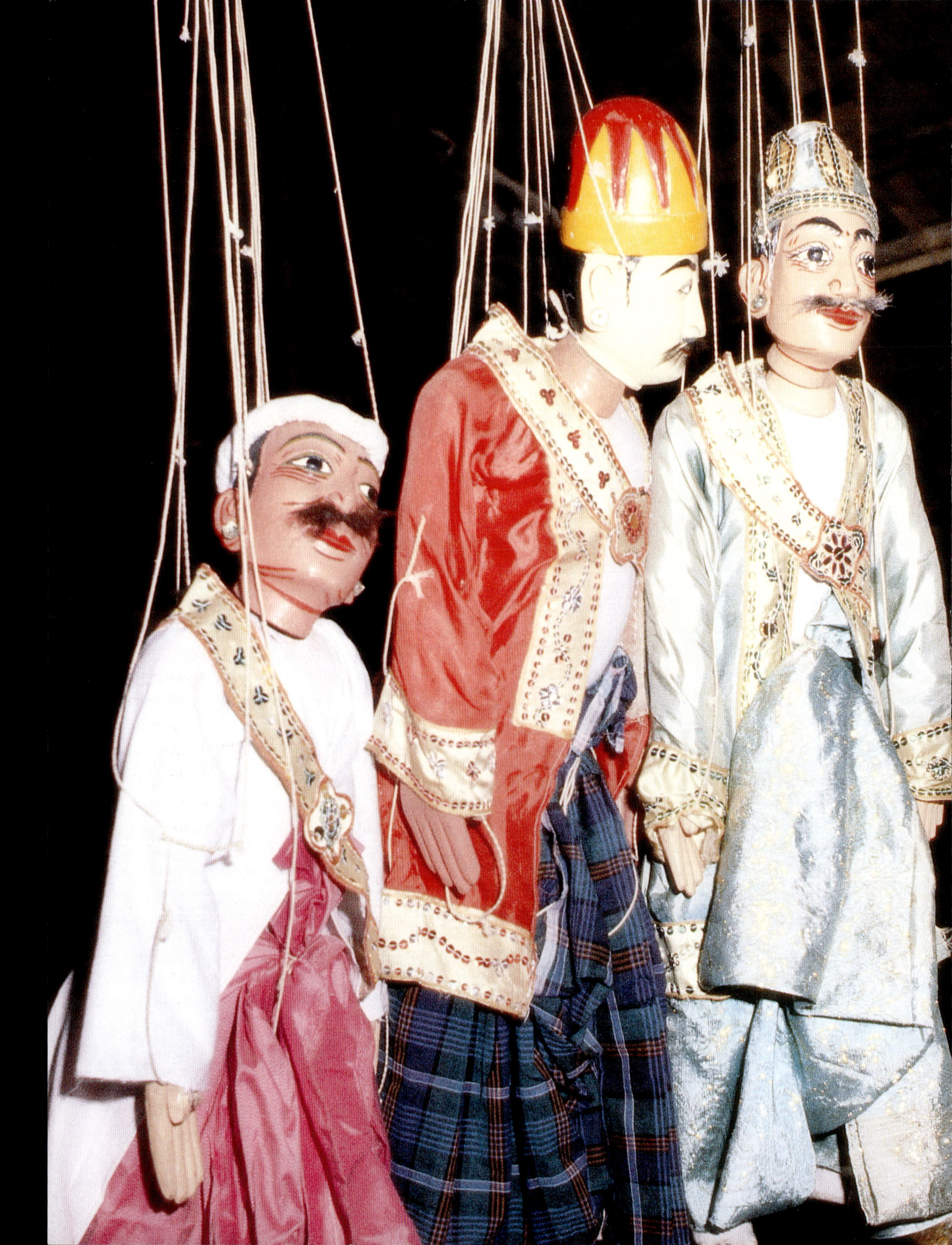

WARD KEELER

Dying Puppets and Living Arts in Burma

In a Thai restaurant I frequent in Austin, Texas, there figure among the usual decorative items in such establishments—photographs of the king and queen of Thailand, generic paintings of boats passing among houses on stilts, pictures of tropical fruits—a number of wooden puppets. They are fairly well crafted, measuring anywhere from one to two feet in height. Vivid expressions are painted on their faces, while jackets and full skirts cover their bodies. Hung by their strings, they smile or scowl, depending on the character, at all who pass by. Presumably, though, few of those restaurant patrons who do glance at them realize that these marionettes are not from Thailand but from its neighbor and longtime rival, Burma. It is a sad fact about the Burmese marionette tradition that its puppets have been sold off in great numbers and now hang lifelessly in shops, restaurants, homes, and a few museums around the world. If the wholesale removal of art objects from any country is ethically questionable, the selling off of puppets is cause for particular regret, since such puppets in their own society are the almost living embodiments of an image of the human world, whereas outside it they are simply decorative objects and souvenirs—that is, dead.

Reports of the imminent demise of Burmese puppets actually started in the late nineteenth century. I spent a year in Burma in 1987–88 in the hopes of learning more about the tradition and discovering whether it really was near extinction. I had previously done research on the Javanese and Balinese shadow play traditions *(wayang kulit)*, still very popular art forms on those two islands of Indonesia. I was interested in finding out why puppet traditions should flourish in that country and yet apparently wither in another, closely related society. Even if Burma, Java, and Bali have each, given their differing histories, come to be linked to diverse religions (namely, Theravada Buddhism, Islam, and Balinese Hinduism, respectively), as Southeast Asian societies all three share many cultural influences. Yet their puppets have encountered widely differing fates.

The year that I was in Burma turned out to be politically tense during the first several months and politically tumultuous in the last few. It was not an ideal time to be looking into performing arts, because fewer performances were held during the "festival season"—the cool months from November through February or March—than would normally have been the case, or so I was told by friends in Mandalay, where I was living. I was still astonished by the number and variety of performances that were put on, sponsored either by Buddhist pagodas for their annual festivals or by city neighborhoods. Throughout the year, there were always a number of movies playing in town and countless video shops showing movies in backrooms. A curfew

■ Modern puppets in Mandalay

imposed after the civic uprising of August 1988 put a stop to large public gatherings, but it did not stop people from moving along alleys and pathways to the nearest video shops even after the eight o'clock signal had sounded.

The advent—and enormous popularity—of movies does nothing to explain the decline of puppets. In Indonesia, puppets and movies flourish side by side. I will offer a few suggestions for why Burmese puppeteers are now so rarely called upon to display their talents, and more regrettably still, are training no young people into their ranks. But I should first recount the vagaries of my efforts to research the topic.

PUPPET TROUPE

I had already been living in Mandalay for a few months when I finally heard where I might find a puppeteer. My language tutor and I went to the neighborhood where he was said to live, near the banks of the Irrawaddy River, and asked after him. His neighbors pointed out his house, and he invited us right in. He was happy to recount stories of when he had first apprenticed to a puppeteer as a young man and how he had moved about the countryside during the festival season with the puppeteer's troupe. He also related some sample stories as they were given in performance. But he explained that the head of the troupe that he had performed with, Shwebo U Tin Maung, had died in 1980, and the troupe had struggled to stay together, finally disbanding only a couple of years after his death. It was, as far as he knew, the last puppet troupe extant. He had heard that the troupe leader's son still had the puppets, but they sat in a box, unused.

He also mentioned that it was too bad that I had not found him sooner, since about a month earlier he and some other veteran performers had been asked to perform for a pagoda festival on the outskirts of town. Research in Southeast Asia, where getting word about performances always seems chancy, has inured me to the sinking sensations word of performances just gone by always causes, but I must say I took that bit of news quite hard.

Nevertheless, I was delighted when the puppeteer invited me to go out to a village north of Mandalay to visit a number of his friends, colleagues from the troupe of Shwebo U Tin Maung who lived there. A full troupe of players, he said, could in the past number as many as twenty or twenty-five people: two principal puppeteers (*cou: hswe: hsaya,* literally, "string-pulling masters"), one of whom manipulated the prince, the other the princess; about twelve people to speak the puppets' parts, some of whom also manipulated the strings for secondary characters; seven musicians; and one or two technicians. While manipulating the puppets, particularly the princess, was technically the most demanding task, it was not the most prestigious or best paid. Instead, the man who spoke the prince's part was looked upon as the most important member of the troupe, followed by the speaker for the princess, and then the clowns.

To a Westerner, it may seem surprising that one person manipulated a puppet while another spoke for it. It is not so surprising in Asia, however. The tradition of Japanese mannequin puppets (Bunraku) makes the same separation between speakers and manipulators. Indonesian shadow puppets combine the speaker's and manipulator's roles, but most Indonesians take the ability to speak in an appropriate and convincing fashion to be a puppeteer's most important skill. Burmese, too, seem to have taken speaking styles as the real focus of the art form, not the puppets' movements in themselves. In fact, the speakers for the puppets sat behind the puppet manipulators and so were unable to see the puppets: it was up to the puller of the strings to make a puppet move in accordance with the speaker's words and songs, rather than the reverse. The singing and speaking styles were highly distinctive and to a considerable degree unique to the marionette tradition, even though most, if not all, the stories in the puppet repertoire were shared with other forms of Burmese theater.

To reach the village where the puppeteer's friends lived, we biked along the main road, then along a canal to a village set among fields planted in sesame. The day was warm, and when we got to the village the five men who joined us sat on mats outside, sipping green tea out of small cups. They appeared to be in their sixties or seventies. Two of them were brothers, and the younger of the two mentioned that his older brother was particularly famous for his ability to speak in the manner of someone who is greatly distressed. Other speakers had equally specific talents. Until about World War II, the men explained, the princess's voice was taken by a male, and the ability to speak in a convincingly feminine fashion was greatly admired.

I asked the men how often they performed, and they said it was very rare and getting rarer. They had indeed performed fairly recently, but that had been their only engagement in more than a year. They found it difficult to put on a performance even when there was a willing sponsor, since no one had a full set of puppets anymore. Someone would have to travel about the region, getting one puppet from here, another from there. And it was the same for the players: they would have to track down everyone they knew who might still be able to perform. As people moved away or died, such performers were getting scarcer.

The men spoke quietly, somewhat wistfully, assuring me that since they were training no younger puppeteers, the art form would die with them. At a certain point, the oldest man present, who had said very little, began to speak. I could not follow all he said but soon began to feel uncomfortable, seeing that he was becoming increasingly upset. As his voice got shriller and his eyes began to well up with tears, I felt sad, embarrassed, and helpless at how to respond. My Burmese, still adequate to the expression of only the most conventional of sentiments, failed me

■ Clown, modern puppet

completely in the face of such intense feeling. Furthermore, this man's sadness seemed all too justified, as the tradition he had known and practiced from childhood seemed fated to die with him.

Suddenly everyone smiled. This was the older brother whose special art lay in his ability to speak in the manner of someone dissolving into tears. I had to agree that he did it very convincingly.

PERFORMANCE

It was after returning to the monastery where I was living that I conceived the idea of sponsoring a performance myself. It seemed clear that if I wished to see what a performance was like, there was no alternative. Granted, I had heard that short performances were given for tourists in a village near the ancient capital of Pagan, a day's trip down the Irrawaddy River. But such performances would tell me little about how a troupe performed for a Burmese audience. So I began making inquiries.

By that time, my wife and I were living in a small wooden house on the outskirts of Mandalay. But for the three months I was in Mandalay before my wife joined me there, I had stayed in a monastery in the city. I was not a monk but rather a lay guest of a very affable and hospitable monk who invited me to stay in a room attached to the late nineteenth-century brick building that housed him, an old man who had recently entered the monkhood, and a novice from the Shan Hills, which lie east of Mandalay. The building was one of several collectively known as the Compound of the Minister of the Horse, that is, the monasteries established by the minister of the cavalry at the end of the last century. A low wall surrounded the whole complex, and there was a finished surface between the building in which I stayed, two adjoining monasteries, and a gate in the wall that led out to a market. It seemed a very good place in which to stage a performance, and my former host kindly agreed to the project.

Burmese attitudes toward the attendance of monks at performances are somewhat mixed. There is an impression, fairly well developed among older members of the *sangha,* or monkhood, that such worldly pleasures as the performing arts are not an appropriate way for individuals devoting their lives to an escape from the vain illusions of this world to spend their time. Not all monks, however, particularly not younger ones, whose commitment to the ascetic style of life is not always so intense, find it contradictory to enjoy some part of a performance in their neighborhood. Monks' lay supporters show the same range of responses, from stern disapproval to indulgent tolerance.

In any case, it is in no way inappropriate for a performance to be held on temple or monastery grounds. Such institutions are not conceived of as set apart from the

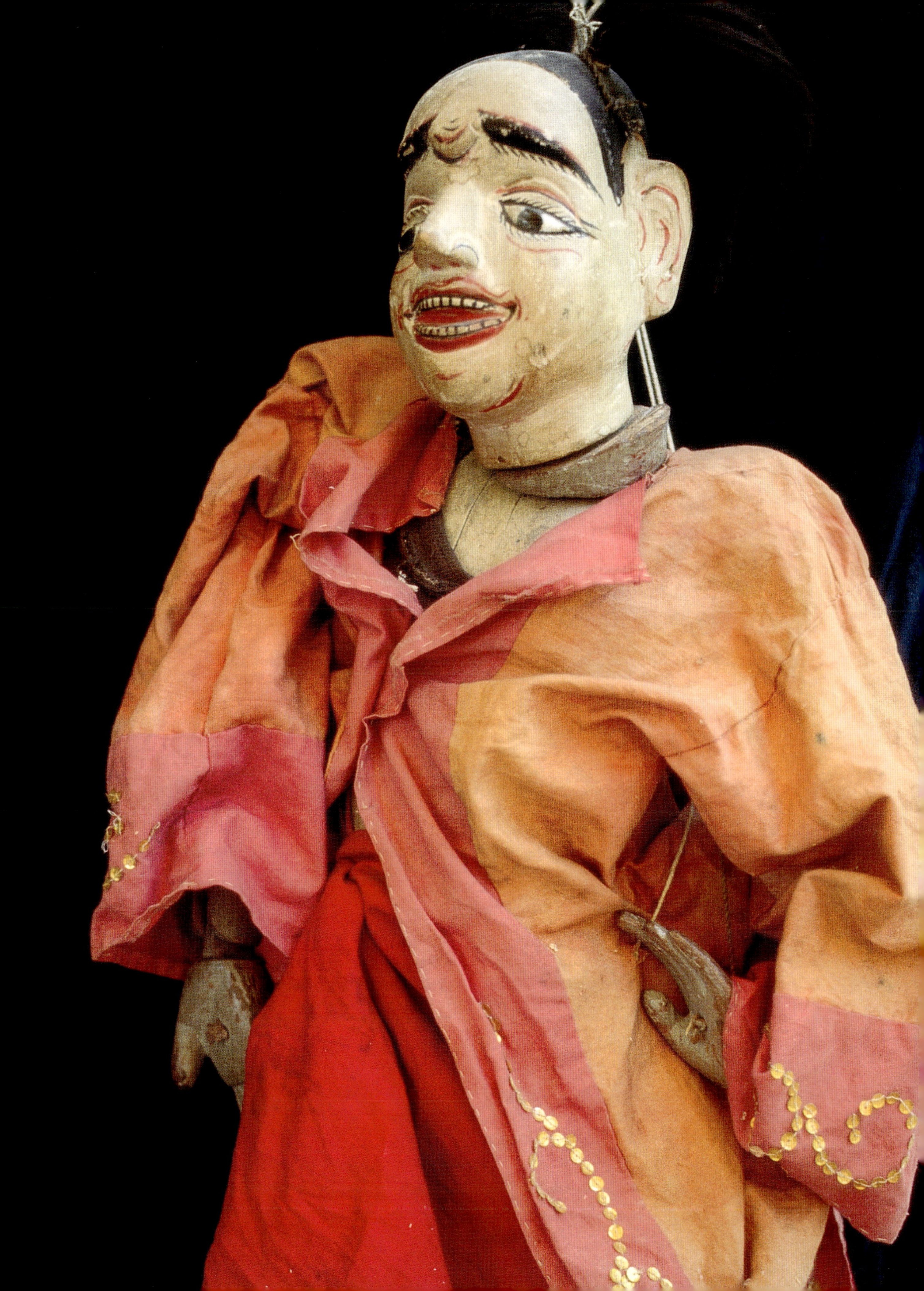

lives of the laity but rather as important parts of their community. True, some monasteries, such as the many that cover the hills of Sagaing, across the Irrawaddy and a bit to the south of Mandalay, are located at a remove from the hustle of town, and deliberately so. They are intended to afford monks the tranquillity conducive to meditation and study. But only some monks opt for such isolation. In town, the close links that bind the monks and the laity mean that traffic between the sangha and the world is constant. It has to be: monks are forbidden to provide for their own livelihood and must depend for their survival on donations of food from lay supporters. At its most severe, this rule means that monks should go out each day to seek alms. In practice, that is only occasionally done. Many monks prefer to let their lay supporters send daily contributions of food to them, routinizing the relationship in such a way as to make it easier on everyone except perhaps the young people—children in the lay supporters' family or novices sent out by the monastery—who must do the running.

I knew that performances could be held on monastery grounds because, not long after I had first moved to the Compound of the Minster of the Horse, an old and venerable monk died. Posters had soon gone up on the compound's gates listing the events that would follow, and among them was a performance of *anyein',* a vaudeville-like form in which three or four male clowns go through joking routines while a female performer sings and dances, all backed up by a band combining Burmese and Western musical instruments. The performance was held, I was told, to enable laypeople to appreciate the auspiciousness of an old monk's death. But the word used in Burmese for the passing of monks is not the one applied to the end of a layperson's life; it expresses rather the perfection attained by a monk, who is sure to go on to some higher form commensurate with the disciplines he accomplished in this world. Indeed, the funeral for the monk was brief and understated, and his body was set to burn at the cremation grounds at the edge of the city with remarkably little ceremony: it happened so fast I nearly missed my ride back to the monastery. The *anyein',* in contrast, went on for several hours, to a delighted audience of neighborhood people.

When I broached the idea of putting on a performance at the monastery, the puppeteer I had first met was very receptive. He arranged with his friends from the village to participate, and among them they organized a troupe of musicians, another string-pulling master (whose technique turned out to be dazzling), and a woman who would, in the more recent fashion, speak for the princess puppet. On the day of the performance, in July, a stage was built in the monastery yard, and by evening the yard was filled with people from the neighborhood and friends I had invited. Some performances in Burma are given for paying audiences, but in the past the usual practice was for the sponsors to give performances for the benefit of a non-paying public. Such was always the case, as far as I know, for puppets. For the many children who attended, this was probably the first puppet performance they had ever seen. Many of their elders remarked that it had been years since they had seen one. There was an air of considerable excitement as people waited for the performance to begin.

The stage was a platform, raised several feet off the ground. On the ground between the audience and the stage were arranged the instruments of the Burmese orchestra, a richly decorated array of drums, tuned gongs, and a woodwind instrument with a peculiar, drooping horn. The presence of several types of gongs clearly relates this orchestra, called the *hsain,* to other Southeast Asian musical ensembles such as Javanese and Balinese *gamelan.* But the speed at which most compositions are played and the reedy sound of the oboelike woodwind instrument call to mind South Asian or even West Asian musical forms as well.

The stage was large, but only a few feet back from the front edge was hung a long piece of cloth, about four feet high and running the full length of the platform. The puppets were made to dance in front of this cloth backdrop. Hanging several feet off the ground and closer to the front of the stage was another long bolt of cloth. The two pieces of cloth combined to conceal the string-pullers from the audience, although occasionally a string-puller's toes could be seen poking forward underneath the lower cloth. In the backstage area, that is, behind the backdrop and the puppet manipulators, sat the people speaking and singing for the puppets. They passed microphones back and forth to each other, their dialogue amplified through old and tinny but still powerful loudspeakers. They did not even bother to look toward the puppets and the front of the stage, knowing that it was the manipulators' responsibility to follow cues.

In the past, a puppet troupe was often engaged for two or three successive nights. The musicians started to play at seven in the evening, the puppets began to dance at nine, and the performance ended at sunrise, about six the next morning. I was sponsoring only one night's performance, but it followed the same set pattern as would have been the case if it had been the first evening of a series. It commenced with music that signaled the threefold destruction of the world. This was followed by the dance of a spirit medium, then the dance of a tiger. A horse danced to pay homage to the spirits, then a monkey danced, and next two ogres appeared and soon fought. (This scene reminded me of a comic meeting of ogres in the *anyein'* I had seen a few months before. But it was the marionette theater that provided the model that other performing arts in Burma have taken on.) Then an alchemist danced, and following him four royal ministers appeared, soon after joined by their king. This scene at the royal court began at about midnight and served as an introduction to the story to be recounted later.

The royal audience ended as the ministers went forth to greet the crown prince on his return from long study in preparation for his future reign. The prince's appearance, accompanied by attendants, led to an extended scene in which he was joined by the princess and her attendants. Never omitted, this scene full of singing and dancing, plus comedy, was generally considered the high point of any puppet performance even though it did nothing to advance the plot.

As is true for virtually all the classical arts I have seen in Southeast Asia, a clear distinction obtained in this scene between the refined, honey-tongued, elegantly attired, and delicately proportioned high-status characters—in this case, the prince and princess—and their large, gruff, crudely dressed, and comical servants. The royal characters sang poetry and danced. Their small limbs—each puppet measured only about six to eight inches in height—moved in perfect time to the music with a kind of boneless agility that has set the standard for all classical dancers in Burma. Their attendants made jokes in gravelly voices and moved antically, to the great amusement of the crowd.

Well, what was left of the crowd. In the course of the performance the number of spectators had dwindled steadily, leaving only a small group of diehards to laugh at the servants and take pleasure in the prince's and princess's superb grace. The lateness of the hour—it was after one by the time the scene started—might appear to explain that fact. But that is not explanation enough, since large crowds will remain much later to watch other kinds of performances, such as the amalgam of dance and melodrama forms called *za' pwe:,* which also go on until dawn, or close to it. Perhaps more people would have come to see the last hour or so of the show, when the story comes to the fore, since sometimes people who have to get up early will stop by to see the tail end of a performance. But the small size of the crowd at two in the morning suggested that puppets had indeed lost their ability to keep Burmese spectators interested.

At close to three, in any case, the question became moot. To my astonishment, I felt a few drops of rain on my head. Mandalay is in a "rain shadow," an area of central Burma cut off by a range of hills from the moisture-laden clouds that roll in from the Bay of Bengal and drench the Arakan coast. As a result, Mandalay receives only a modest amount of rainfall each year, most of it falling in May and June. At the time of the performance I had sponsored, in July, it had not rained in weeks. But there it was. The troupe's response was instantaneous. Everything came to a halt, and the puppets were rushed inside, people exclaiming that even small amounts of rain would ruin the puppets. The stage, as well, was dissassembled in short order.

I was dismayed at this sudden shift in my fortunes. Granted, I was exhausted. But I was anxious to see how a story was told, and the story in a puppet performance does not really start until about three. I was all the more distressed because the rain actually never came: a few more drops fell but that was all. The monk in whose monastery I had stayed smiled and said that the rain had not really posed such a threat. Instead, he said, these were old men, and they were happy to seize on an excuse to stop performing when their stamina was giving out. He may well have been right. On the other hand, some of the players seemed to be warming to things as the "two figures dancing" (the scene with the prince and princess) progressed.

My efforts to research Burmese puppets largely ended there. It was only a few weeks later that the country erupted in large-scale unrest, on the fateful eighth day of the eighth month of 1988 (8/8/88). Those events of course changed the tenor of my conversations with people. But I am left wondering whether there is any way to account for the disparities between those performing arts that win large audiences in Burma today and Burmese puppets, which arouse such little interest but were once enormously popular.

That puppets were once so popular is attested to by the considerable amount of royal patronage they enjoyed. It is said that at the time of the last royal court in Mandalay, in the late nineteenth century, King Thibaw and his queen each included among their retainers an entire puppet troupe. In contrast, when the two state-run academies for the arts were established in Rangoon and Mandalay after World War II, music and dance were included among their departments, but not puppetry.

It is perhaps worth stressing just how enthusiastically the Burmese public supports other types of performances. I have mentioned the vaudeville-like *anyein'*, which lasts for a few hours, and the larger-scale *za'pwe:,* which continues until dawn. Block associations and pagoda festival committees often put on the latter, building large sheds to house the stage and the spectators. (Sometimes troupes set up a shed themselves and charge admission in a commercial run.) A *za'pwe:* often starts with a group of young women and girls, perhaps six to ten of them, all in matching Burmese dress, dancing identical movements to the accompaniment of both traditional Burmese and electronic Western instruments. A series of pop singers then appear on stage, dressed in Western clothes, to sing current hits. A play set in the present lasts from about eleven at night until about three. Then a traditional tale is usually played, in old-fashioned Burmese dress, lasting until dawn. However, some troupes have dispensed with this part of the performance, extending the modern dress play a bit later and then having the starring male dancers dance and sing in displays of their virtuosity with an array of female dancers.

MOVIES AND OTHER ARTS

And then there are movies. In Rangoon as well as in Mandalay, I was often astonished to see long lines of people waiting to get into movie theaters—in the morning or afternoon, not just at night. In a climate as hot as Burma's, and without air conditioning or even fans, the inside of a movie theater was to me an apt vision of hell. Burmese are clearly not put off. And as I have mentioned, large theaters are not the only venue in which movies can be seen. Middle-class Burmese can see them on state-run television or on videocassette recorders, and a burgeoning number of video shops show films in small rooms, often two or three a night. The titles are the usual run of Western action and horror films, the very popular kung fu movies, and a few Burmese movies (although these tend to run more often in the large theaters), mostly melodramas. By 1988, I was told that the government's store of foreign exchange was so depleted that it could no longer purchase color film, and so Burmese films were back to being made in black and white.

Pagoda and neighborhood festivals also often screen movies as one of their

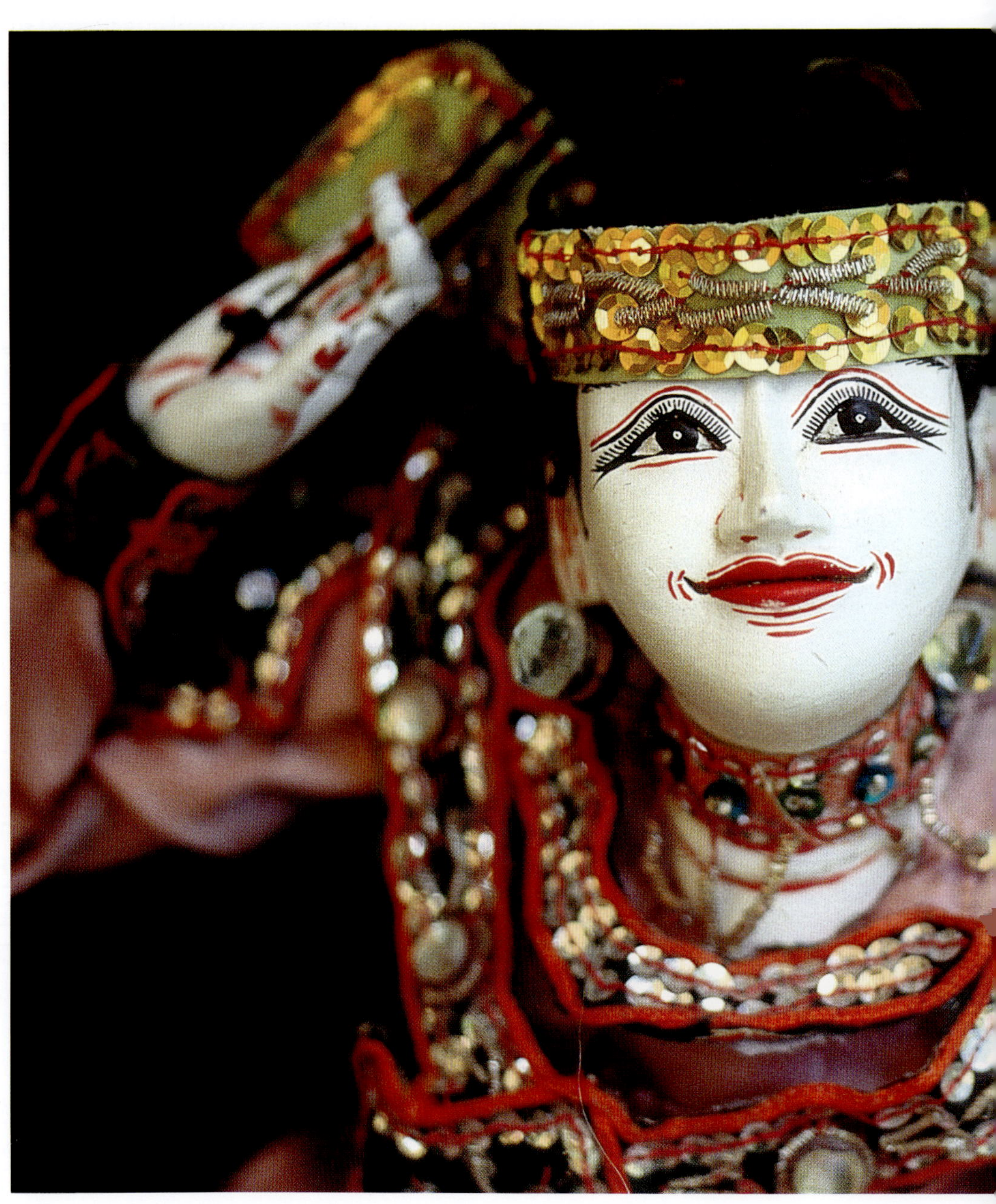

■ Min:tha: (prince), modern puppet

entertainments. The choice of fare is eclectic. At one pagoda festival, an unusually large crowd gathered round a video monitor to watch what turned out to be a Japanese soft-core pornography film. When the sex scenes started, the audience got to see a few seconds' worth of female nudity. Then the film was fast-forwarded to the next scene, while the audience hooted.

Pornographic films are not shown in large theaters, but they are a staple part of the video shops' showings, smuggled into the country, like so much else, across the Thai border. While all pornographic films are forbidden by the Burmese government, in fact the showing of foreign pornography seems to evoke few sanctions. I was told, however, that anyone found to have a hand in the production of a pornographic film in Burma was put to death. I have no idea whether that claim is true. That friends of mine believed it points up what I think is a fairly widespread attitude in Southeast Asia: that pornography is something that concerns foreigners, and that it's fine for males to watch it, as long as it does not confuse them about principles of moral conduct in their own society.

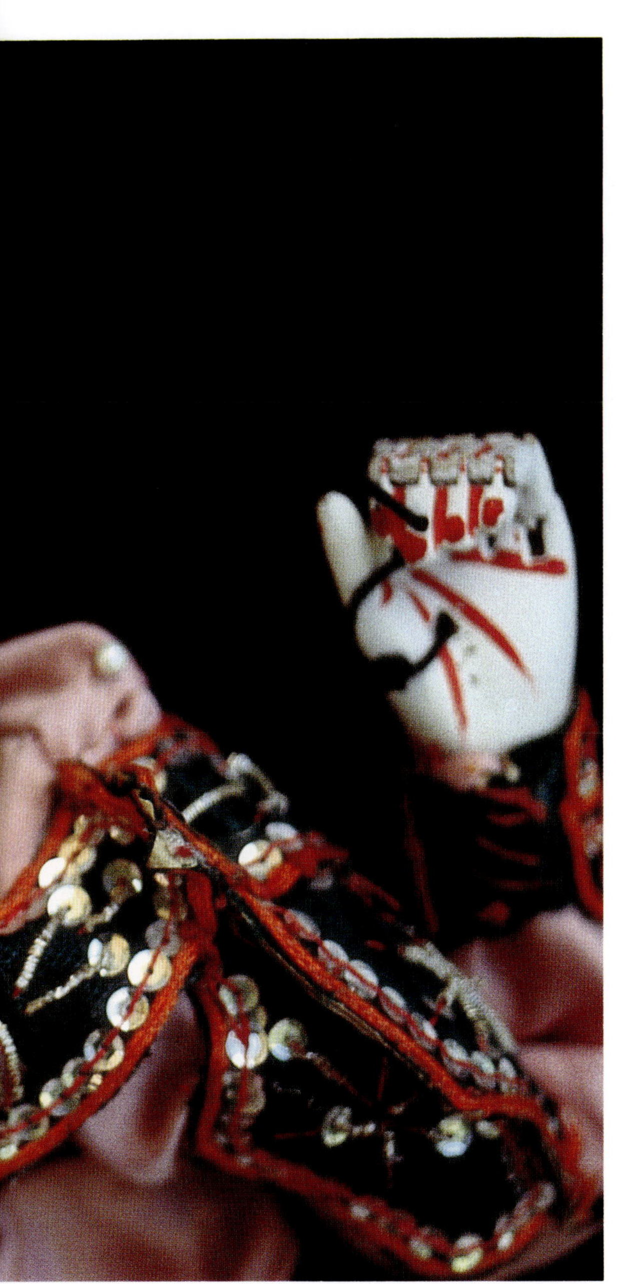

Vaudeville, drama, pop-music concerts, dance, and films—Burmese attend a variety of kinds of performances with great frequency. Why, then, have puppets lost their allure? No single explanation suffices, but a number of points may help to account for their near disappearance. Relative expense, the nature of arts patronage, and the contents of the stories all conspire to make puppets ill-suited to contemporary Burmese society.

A puppet troupe is larger than an *anyein'* troupe and therefore more expensive to sponsor. On some occasions, therefore, putting on a performance of *anyein'* may be the most financially attractive option. However, the most expensive genre of all to stage is the still very popular *za'pwe:*. These performances are mounted before paying audiences, and if puppets were still truly popular, no doubt they could also be performed commercially. As a matter of fact, I did once see a commercial performance of puppets at a pagoda festival in Rangoon. But they were hand-held puppets, and they performed comedy and pop singing with a bit of moralizing against the consumption of alcohol—a far cry from the classical marionette repertoire.

Rather than stress financial considerations, I would point to the matter of sponsorship. I assume that the royal family, and other members of the aristocracy, sponsored puppet plays in the past, as the presence of two puppet troupes at Thibaw's court attests. At present, however, private families in town do not sponsor performances, at least not beyond inviting a few popular singers, and maybe a dancer, to perform at weddings. Instead, the sponsorship of large-scale entertainments is by committee; the organizers of a festival decide what kinds of entertainment to sponsor. In any society, patrons of the arts define themselves as they select the arts and artists they support. They seek to elevate the impression of their own aesthetic discernment—and in the process, their social status—by demonstrating the classical purity or refinement of their tastes. But members of a committee do not see their own status at stake in their choice of genres. They seek to attract and entertain large audiences by whatever means they think will be most effective. Their own family's tastes are not at issue, only the success of the festival, a success defined in large part by how many people are attracted to the events.

INDONESIAN SHADOW PLAY

The contrast in this regard between Java and Bali on the one hand and Burma on the other is telling. Shadow plays in both Indonesian societies are highly comical, and the mythological stories they relate often fade into the background as servants, monsters, and evil knights engage in long, and hilarious, battles. Yet the genre retains its cachet as the most ancient, most venerable, and most prestigious of the performing arts in Java and Bali. To sponsor a shadow play is to take on the mantle of the upholder of "traditional" Javanese or Balinese culture, something that redounds well on a person's or a family's status. In contemporary Burma, at least in town, private sponsorship of performances simply does not come up as a way to enhance or substantiate a family's claims to high status. So the incentive to maintain a puppet tradition as a kind of museum piece, by means of which a sponsor—like a donor to a famous collection in the West—keeps his name associated to all that is "best" in society, does not exist.

Still, the fact that Burmese families do not invest in their status through the sponsorship of classical arts does not explain why a festival committee would turn away from puppets as a way to attract crowds. In Indonesia, institutions sponsor shadow plays to mark such events as the opening of a new building or the anniversary of a department's formation, and they do so in the knowledge that if they engage a famous puppeteer great crowds will gather. Even though marionettes in Burma are not cheap to sponsor and do not provide a means to enhance one's status, they would still prosper if they were to the public's taste. So we must still address the question of why marionettes no longer engage the interest of most Burmese.

PUBLIC TASTE

I would suggest that Burmese society has changed in ways that make the very conservative and classical puppet theater less compelling to people than other forms of entertainment. Everything about the puppet plays bespeaks an aesthetic sense very much linked to the deeply hierarchical nature of precolonial Burmese society. The focus on courtly life, the reliance on a courtly style, and above all the sheer conservatism of the genre, all appear to make the puppets no longer relevant to a society that has left its aristocratic traditions behind.

Performing arts, to win their spectators' attention, need not mirror spectators' lives in any straightforward way. But they should somehow relate to people's experience and fantasies. Burmese today feel no connection to the elaborate etiquette and studied grace of the aristocrats that are the focus of most puppet plays, and perhaps that helps to explain the genre's eclipse. Burma contrasts with both Java and Bali in this regard, for in those two Indonesian societies the status distinctions that shaped the tenor of human interaction in the past continue to preoccupy people today. Indeed, it is in those areas of Java closest to the old court centers of Jogjakarta and Surakarta that shadow plays have always been most popular. Even though the Javanese aristocracy no longer wields any political power, its prestige—and the notion of spiritual potency that shored up that prestige—continue to exercise a great hold on the thinking of many Javanese. The complex Balinese amalgam of Indic and Polynesian understandings of social organization makes the distribution of titles and prestige in that society the stuff of endless machinations, not unlike the way characters in shadow plays maneuver for advantage.

However, the historical and religious subjects that made up the bulk of the repertoire in Burmese puppet plays might still hold some allure for Burmese, despite the aristocratic bias in their contents, if the genre were not so extremely conservative in its actual performance practice. In Indonesian shadow plays, an invariant structure provides all performances with a predictable shape, and both Javanese and Balinese performances begin with long, slow-moving introductions that are largely unintelligible to most members of the audience. Within forty minutes or so, however, a particular story begins to take shape, and dramatic and comic exchanges among characters engage the audience's attention. In the case of Burmese puppets, the first several hours of the play are set, and only the most committed aficionado would be likely to sit through this long opening very many times. In the past, perhaps, it was feasible to relax and socialize during the first few hours. Or perhaps some people came late to performances and enjoyed the songs, humor, and dancing of the scene with the prince and princess and all or part of the story that develops after that scene, just as in Java today many spectators come to a shadow play only at the time the introductory scene is coming to a close. But the Burmese genre seems not to have adapted the structure of its performances to a different context, one in which spectators might demand greater novelty and engagement earlier in the evening.

Indeed, perhaps the most striking contrast between puppet plays and Burma's other performing arts is the degree to which the latter are open to innovation and the former are not. The contrast becomes clear when listening to the musical accompaniment to different performances. Whereas the marionette theater retains a fully Burmese orchestra, most other genres mix Burmese and Western instruments in an altogether improbable fashion. At a *za'pwe:,* for example, the Burmese ensemble will begin to play a composition. After a bit, electric guitars, snare drums, electric keyboard, trumpets, and even trombones, all hooked up to enormous loudspeakers, will either replace the Burmese ensemble or simply join in, completely drowning it out. Then after a little while, the Burmese instruments will play alone again. I admit that I do not find the combination to my taste—it sounds like the musical equivalent of a Mack truck running down a deer. But to many Burmese it must sound like the best of both worlds. In much the same way, a *za'pwe:'s* contents, combining classical dance steps, melodrama, pop songs, old stories, and the twist, abandon all notion of artistic purity in favor of novel and engaging pastiche. The puppet tradition has resisted such divergence from its own conventions, but at the price of losing its audience.

The Japanese have rescued the once extremely popular, but now almost forgotten, genre of mannequin puppets by means of government subsidy. The Burmese government has shown no inclination to do the same for its puppet tradition, and I find I must join the series of writers who have predicted its imminent end. Artificial resuscitation may prove possible, but it is hard to imagine that the standards of performance could be retained when the living masters of the art are all old men without pupils. So instead of encountering Burmese marionettes dancing with energetic grace in the night air of Upper Burma, we will be left to glance at them—motionless—while we choose between one or another Thai curry. ■

FURTHER READING

Htin Aung, U. *Burmese Drama: A Study, with Translations of Burmese Plays.* London: Oxford University Press, 1957

A general introduction to the Burmese theater.

Sein, Kenneth, and J. A. Withey. *The Great Po Sein: A Chronicle of the Burmese Theater.* Bloomington: Indiana University Press, 1965.

A lively account of one of the great stars, and innovators, of the *za'pwe:* tradition.

Singer, Noel. *Burmese Puppets.* Singapore: Oxford University Press, 1992.

The only extended treatment of the subject published in English; beautifully illustrated and containing a wealth of information on the history and performance practice of the Burmese puppet tradition.

■ Ward Keeler is an anthropologist specializing in expressive culture. He has conducted research in Indonesia and Burma; the research on which this article was based was supported by a Fulbright postdoctoral research grant and a grant from the Social Science Research Council. He has published two books on the Javanese shadow play: *Javanese Shadow Plays, Javanese Selves* (Princeton University Press, 1987), and *Javanese Shadow Puppets* (Oxford University Press, 1992). Associate professor of anthropology at the University of Texas at Austin, he is currently visiting lecturer at the Australian National University.

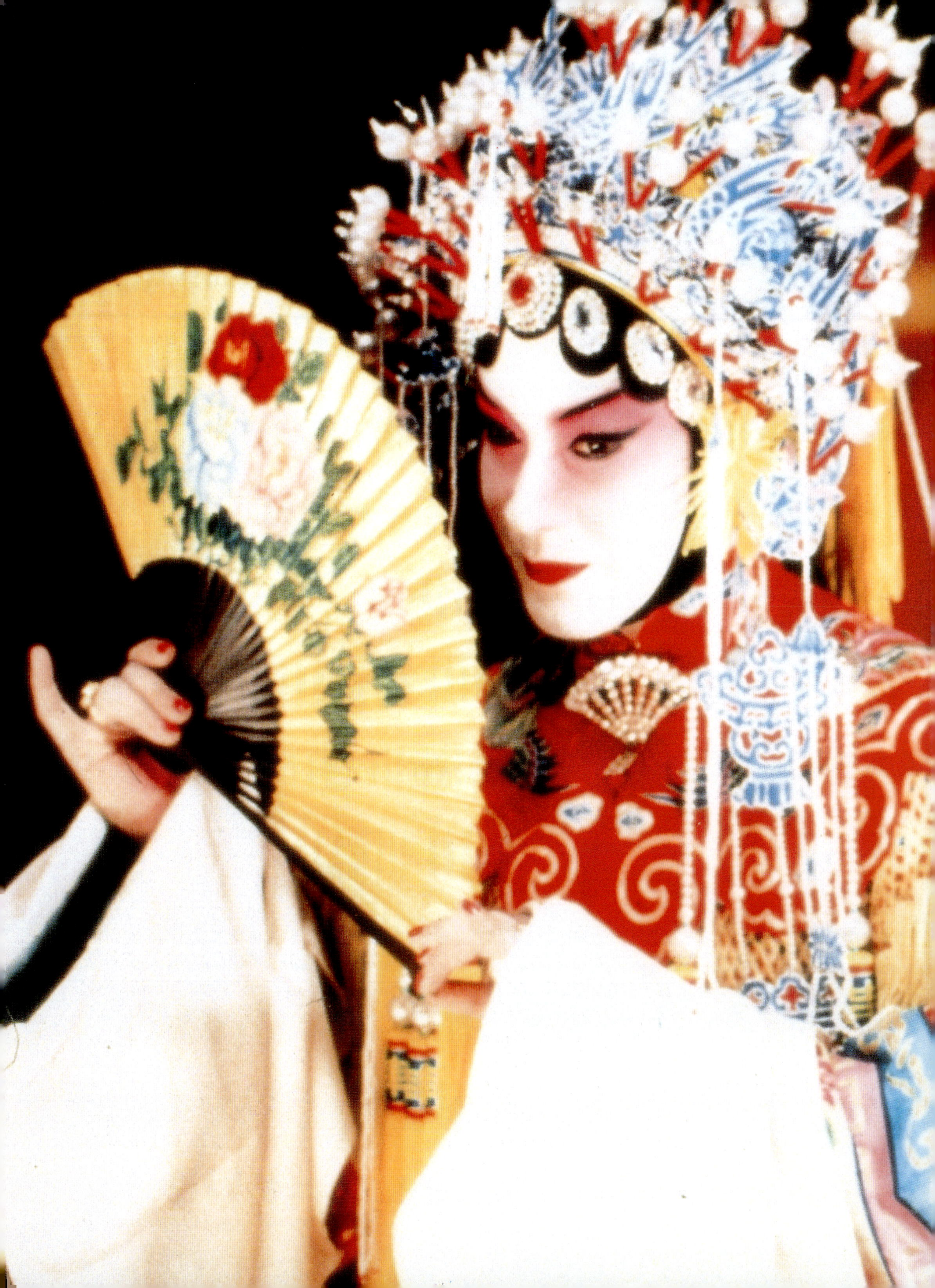

SCARLET CHENG

I Heard a Voice from My Memory Chinese Opera and Film

The first film ever made in China was a celluloid recording of the Beijing opera *Dingjun Mountain,* produced in 1905 by the Feng Tai Photography Shop in Beijing. This is hardly surprising, as Chinese opera was the leading dramatic form at the time, not the spoken dialogue play au courant in the West. In the United States and Europe, the earliest motion pictures had derived from popular stage drama and reflected conventions of heavy pancake makeup, broad gestures, and melodramatic plots.

For the first half of this century, opera remained the dominant form of theatrical expression in China. (Of course, it was also popular in the other two Chinas—Hong Kong and Taiwan—in native dialects. In Taiwan, there also has been a strong tradition of opera performed by puppets.) *Huaju,* the spoken drama form popularized between the two world wars, tried to introduce more naturalistic acting and contemporary themes, but somehow Chinese opera remained the signature theatrical form of the country.

Others have written about the relationship between literature and film, as well as *huaju* and film, but surprisingly little has been written about the relationship between Chinese opera and film. Of course, there have been numerous movie renditions of Chinese opera, especially in the 1950s and 1960s, but I would like to suggest that both the form and the spirit of Chinese opera inform popular Chinese film of other genres as well.

By Chinese opera, I refer to the formally sung and staged operas performed in the various Chinese dialects, highly stylized in presentation, with stories based on history and on classical literature. My primary reference is specifically to Beijing and to Cantonese opera, with which I am most familiar and which those in the West are most likely to see.

I approach the subject as a film writer and not as an opera expert. Like film director Ann Hui, I saw opera (both Beijing opera and Taiwanese opera, in my case) as a child, often staged outdoors during various religious festivals and celebrations in Taipei in the 1950s and 1960s as well as in theaters and on television. Unlike Hui, I did not see many filmed versions of operas, although I did see a number of films in the *huangmei diao* style, an operetta genre that was popularized by the Hong Kong and Taiwan movie studios in the 1960s.

What are some of the connections I began to notice over the years? First, a significant number of actors and filmmakers received opera training, came from opera families, or were great fans of opera. Second, in the martial arts movie revival of the

■ Leslie Cheung, who plays Cheng Dieyi, performs the role of the concubine in Chen Kaige's award-winning film *Farewell My Concubine* (1993).

last two years, we see once more the fascination with acrobatics and movement so evident in Chinese opera. Many movements and poses in the movies echo those of opera. Third, Chinese movies, especially the highly commercial ones of Hong Kong, continue to tell stories symbolically, with simple story lines, in the style of Chinese opera. Fourth, the characters in both theatrical forms tend to be types.

It would take a much longer essay to deal with these subjects adequately, and here I mainly want to introduce some of the connections. I have written little about the musical and the costuming connections, although some opera conventions of music and dress are used in films. We may hear, for example, the deep roll of drums that announces war, the clappers for impending action, a wistful melody on the *erhu* (a two-stringed musical instrument) to evoke sadness or melancholy—all elements in Chinese opera.

Visually, we occasionally see film actors dressed in the flamboyant style of opera, as in two of 1993's top Hong Kong films, *Dong Cheng Xi Jiu* and *The Flirting Scholar,* both farcical period comedies. Shirley Chan, the costume designer for the latter, readily admitted in an interview with me, "I made the costumes brighter in color, the fabrics shinier, more in keeping with stage conventions of opera." To execute the long gowns and hats, she commissioned a Hong Kong tailor who specialized in opera costuming.

CHINESE OPERA

Some believe that the golden age of Chinese theater took place during the Yuan dynasty (1279–1368), but there is a more direct relationship between Chinese opera as we know it today and *kunqu,* a musical drama that arose during the Ming dynasty (1368–1644). Beijing opera appeared in the Qing dynasty (1644–1911), during the late eighteenth and early nineteenth centuries, arising from a combination of Anhui and Hubei opera styles. It became the popular entertainment of both the masses and the ruling class, performed throughout the year at temples, in courtyards, and in other public spaces during celebrations and religious festivals.

The plots turned around exploits of valiant heroes or stories of tragic love, taken from history and from classical literature or, often, from history embroidered with literary imagination. The story line was kept simple, with clear and unmistakable moral themes, usually emphasizing such Confucian values as filial piety, devotion to one's family, loyalty to one's superiors, and so on. Sets and props were kept to an absolute minimum. Instead, much emphasis was placed on the singing and performing of the actors.

Audiences were familiar with the stories, and the specific makeup and costume of the actors signaled the type of character they were playing. For the characters requiring the colorful face painting we identify closely with Beijing opera, the designated colors and patterns held particular significance, such as bravery and loyalty or treachery and connivance. Just as many of the props were symbolic—a horsewhip in hand meant riding—so many of the characters were also symbolic. In fact, middle-aged male and female actors could play the roles of coquettish young women so long as they could assume the voice and the movements of such a part. The art form has remained popular to this century. New librettos continued to be written, though again based on traditional sources.

With the communist takeover of mainland China in 1949, all art forms felt a chill, as they were now expected to serve state interests. The film industry was completely nationalized in 1953, while the performance of Chinese opera, with its "decadent" histories and romances and its reputation for harboring "decadent" social elements, was curtailed. With the Cultural Revolution (1966–76), opera came to a halt; only the sanctioned "revolutionary operas" like *Taking Tiger Mountain by Strategy* and *The Red Lantern* were permitted to be performed.

Meanwhile, in the "other" Chinas of Hong Kong and Taiwan, opera lived on, and opera schools continued to train actors from a tender age in the rigors of voice

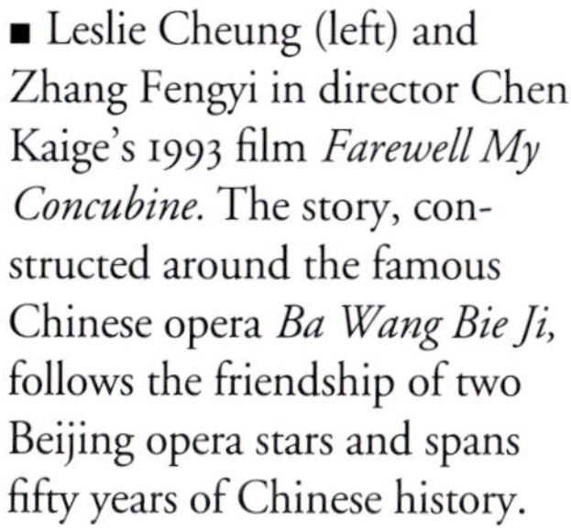

■ Leslie Cheung (left) and Zhang Fengyi in director Chen Kaige's 1993 film *Farewell My Concubine.* The story, constructed around the famous Chinese opera *Ba Wang Bie Ji,* follows the friendship of two Beijing opera stars and spans fifty years of Chinese history.

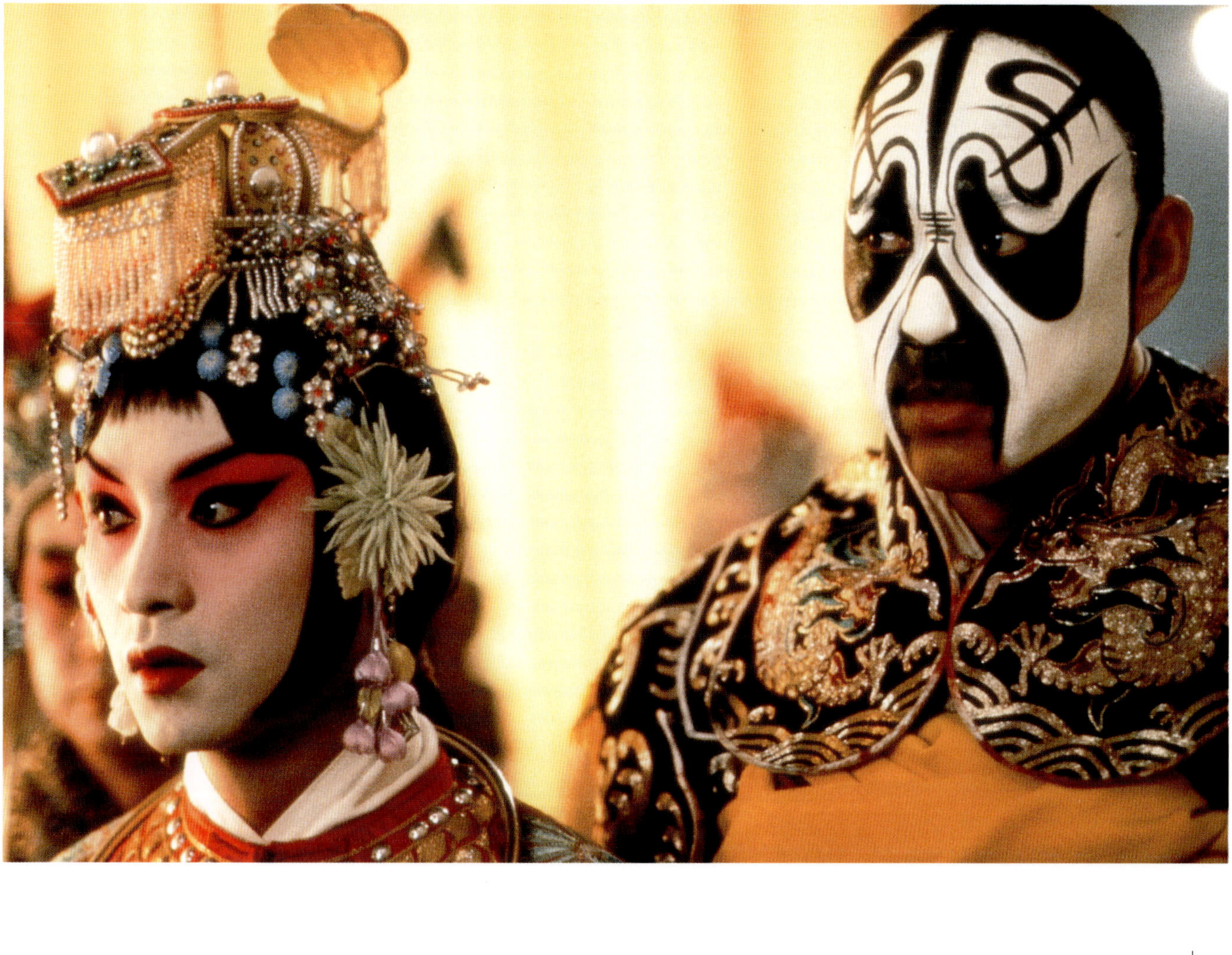

■ In this dramatic composite from the poster for *Farewell My Concubine,* a wounded Juxian is held by her husband, Duan Xiaolou, who is in costume for his role as the king in the opera that gives the film its Chinese title.

and body. In the period after World War II, Chinese operas were often put on film. More than five hundred opera films were made in Hong Kong in the 1950s, accounting for more than one-third of all films in Cantonese dialect. When television became mass entertainment, Chinese opera became a regular staple of the small screen.

Since the end of the Cultural Revolution, opera has had a revival in China,

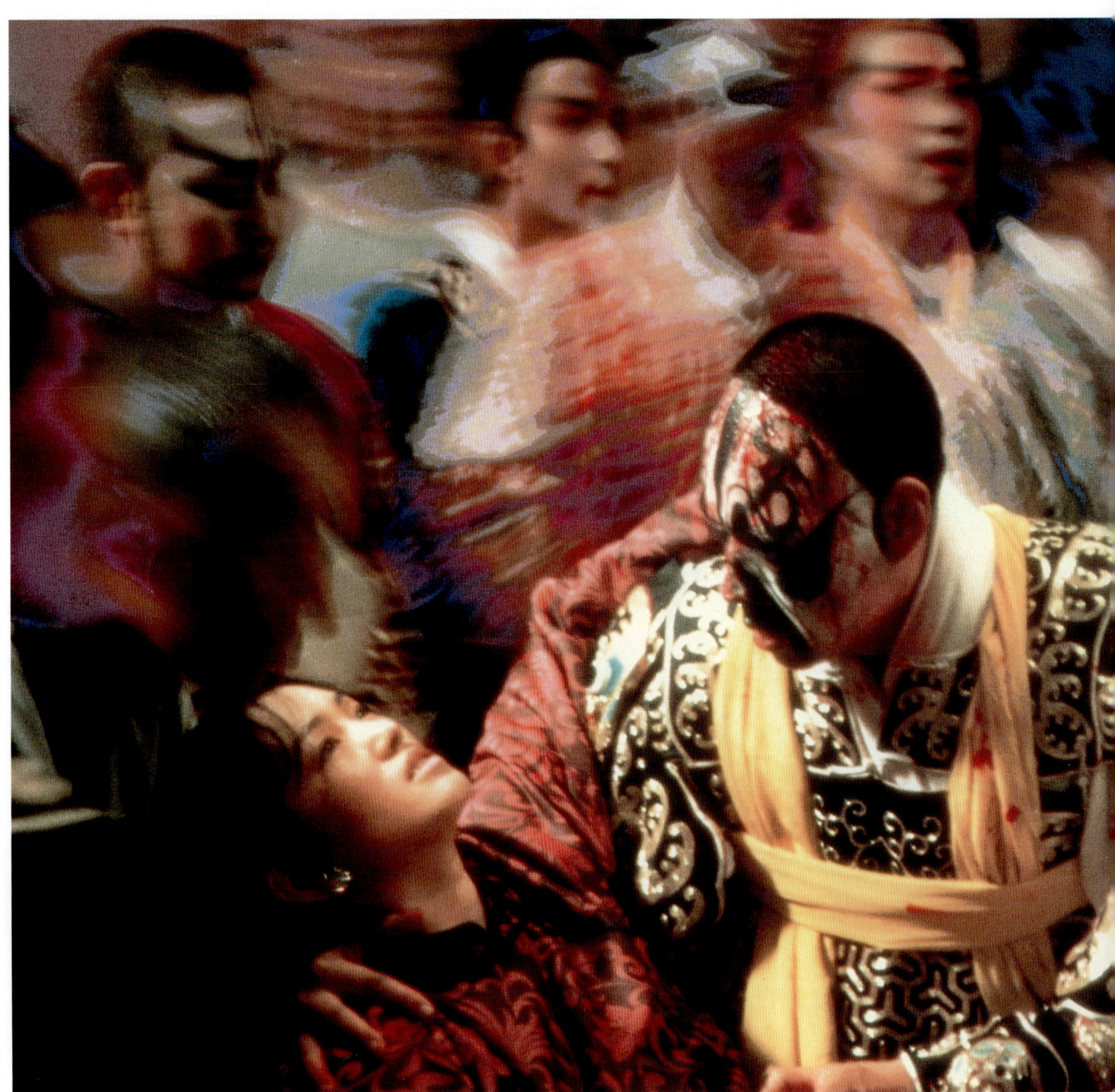

though it is now enjoyed mainly by the older generation and little appreciated by the young. Nevertheless, it influenced an entire generation of filmmakers "because there is something about Chinese opera," as Chen Kaige, director of the award-winning *Farewell My Concubine,* said to me in a recent interview, "that is fundamentally Chinese."

Again, my point of reference is film and filmmakers, and in exploring my theme, I have focused on three feature-length motion pictures, made within the last fourteen years, that are about Chinese opera and opera performers. They are Stanley Kwan's *Rouge* (1988), Ann Hui's *Spooky Bunch* (1980), and Chen Kaige's *Farewell My Concubine* (1993).[1]

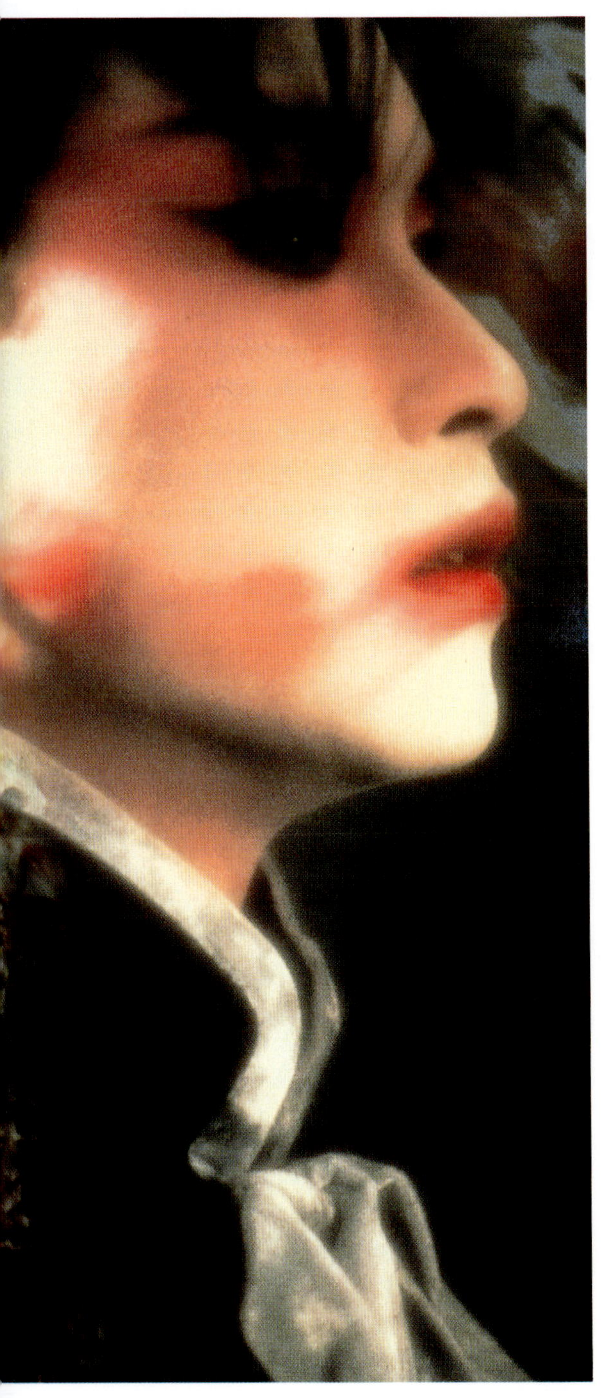

I interviewed these directors for this essay, and what they had to say about themselves and the making of their movies was invaluable to my research and my own understanding. All are of an age—mid-thirties to mid-forties—to have grown up seeing opera performed live and know it as part of daily life, not the exotic and remote institution it is to today's youth.

Furthermore, it seems to me that these directors represent three kinds of exposure to Chinese opera. Stanley Kwan, who grew up in Hong Kong, became a Cantonese opera fan as a child, frequenting performances with his mother and even learning whole scenes from his favorite operas by heart. Ann Hui, who also grew up in Hong Kong, was taken to opera frequently and later watched Cantonese opera films, but she does not describe herself as a fan. Chen Kaige grew up in Beijing, where his father was a movie director who made film versions of Chinese opera and his schoolmate was a grandson of Mei Lanfang (1894–1961), an actor specializing in female roles and whose name was virtually synonymous with Beijing opera.

THE RIGORS OF TRAINING

Of course, these three films are not the only ones in the past two decades to have taken Chinese opera and opera performers as their subject. Many such films reflect a fascination with the rigorous training and discipline requirements of the art. One of the most charming is *Painted Faces* (1989), directed by Hong Kong's Alex Law. It is about the training of young boys for Beijing opera in Hong Kong in the 1960s, a decade of rapid change in the territory.

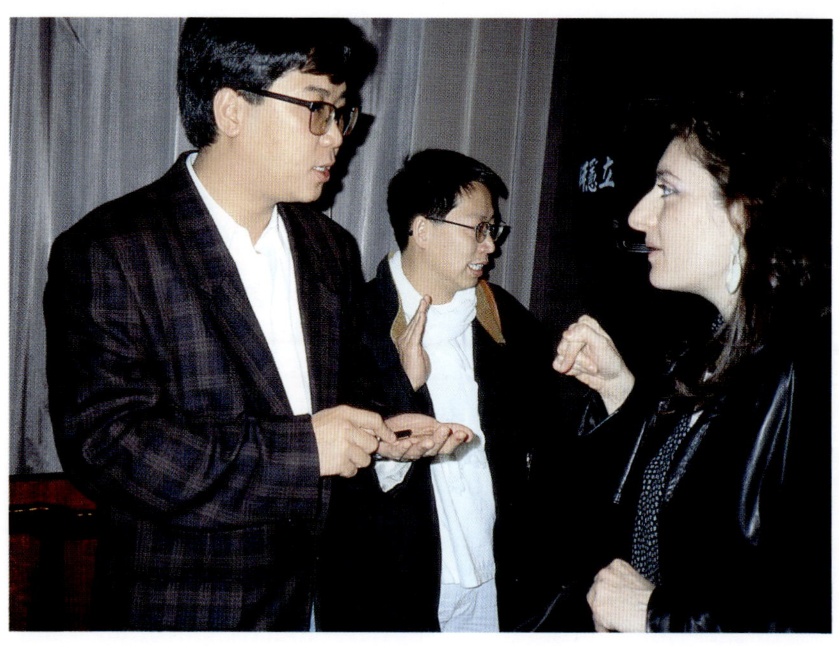

■ Director Stanley Kwan (left) at a film festival

"I always liked Beijing opera," Alex Law has said, "and I have read many autobiographies of opera actors. . . . I approached Samo Hung to play Yu Tsim-yuen [the opera master]. The *Seven Little Treasures* supplied the anecdotes."[2] The "seven little treasures" referred to in the Chinese title of the film are real people—Samo Hung, Jackie Chan, and their classmates who trained in the same Hong Kong opera school and later became film actors and filmmakers. Alex Law and Mabel Cheung, his wife, scripted the film from their experiences.

In addition to acting in movies, Samo Hung also directs them, specializing in action sequences in martial arts films, such as the recently completed *Dong Xie Xi Du* (Evil East, Poisonous West) (1994). His former classmate Jackie Chan is famous for his incredible daredevil stunts in such films as *Police Story* (1985) and sequels. He also produces films for his film company Golden Harvest, one of the biggest in Hong Kong.

In *Painted Faces* we see that training for Chinese opera began young, with boys signed up for demanding and rigorous apprenticeships of several years, during which they practiced stances, movements, and recitations and sang from dawn to dusk. Although the boys are occasionally struck and sent to bed without supper, Master Yu is essentially a decent and compassionate man.

A less benign view is taken by Chen Kaige in *Farewell My Concubine.* The film's first half hour is devoted to the training (in the late 1920s) of Cheng Dieyi and Duan Xiaolou, who will go on to become stars of the Beijing opera world. The boys at this opera school are forced to do grueling exercises, stand in strenuous positions for hours, and bend in extreme extensions. They are humiliated and beaten for minor infractions of the school code, with the teachers taking sadistic pleasure in the punishments. As director Chen points out, the term for training for opera is *da xi,* which means "beating in opera."

STANLEY KWAN: OPERA AFICIONADO

Rouge (1988), directed by Stanley Kwan, is one of the most notable art films to come out of Hong Kong in recent years. It stars the eminently bankable Anita Mui and

Leslie Cheung, both of whom transited to the movies after successful careers as pop singers. Here, Anita Mui plays Fleur, a highly paid courtesan of the 1920s who sings for dinner guests and keeps rich men, like Twelfth Master (Leslie Cheung), company. The young and handsome Twelfth Master falls in love with Fleur, attracted first by her singing a plaintive ballad while dressed in male attire, then by her willowy ways in female attire.

Suddenly, we are fast-forwarded to 1980s Hong Kong, where the unaged Fleur appears at the classified sales office of a newspaper. She asks the clerk to put in a "missing person" notice—for someone who has been dead sixty years. The clerk befriends her, even after learning that she is a ghost. His own rather offhand relationship with his girlfriend, a tough newspaper reporter, is contrasted with Fleur's dreamy romanticism.

In flashback, Fleur is rejected by her lover's family as being beneath them. (Opera performers were once considered on the same level as prostitutes and beggars.) Twelfth Master himself aspires to be a Chinese opera performer, and he leaves his wealthy family to live with Fleur. He takes up opera training, undergoing the humbling experience of starting as a supernumerary. As he explains to the opera master, "I want to do opera, not business." But society has no place for the couple

■ In Stanley Kwan's tragic romance *Rouge* (1988), courtesan Fleur (Anita Mui) accompanies her lover Twelfth Master (Leslie Cheung), to his debut as a supernumerary in a performance of Chinese opera.

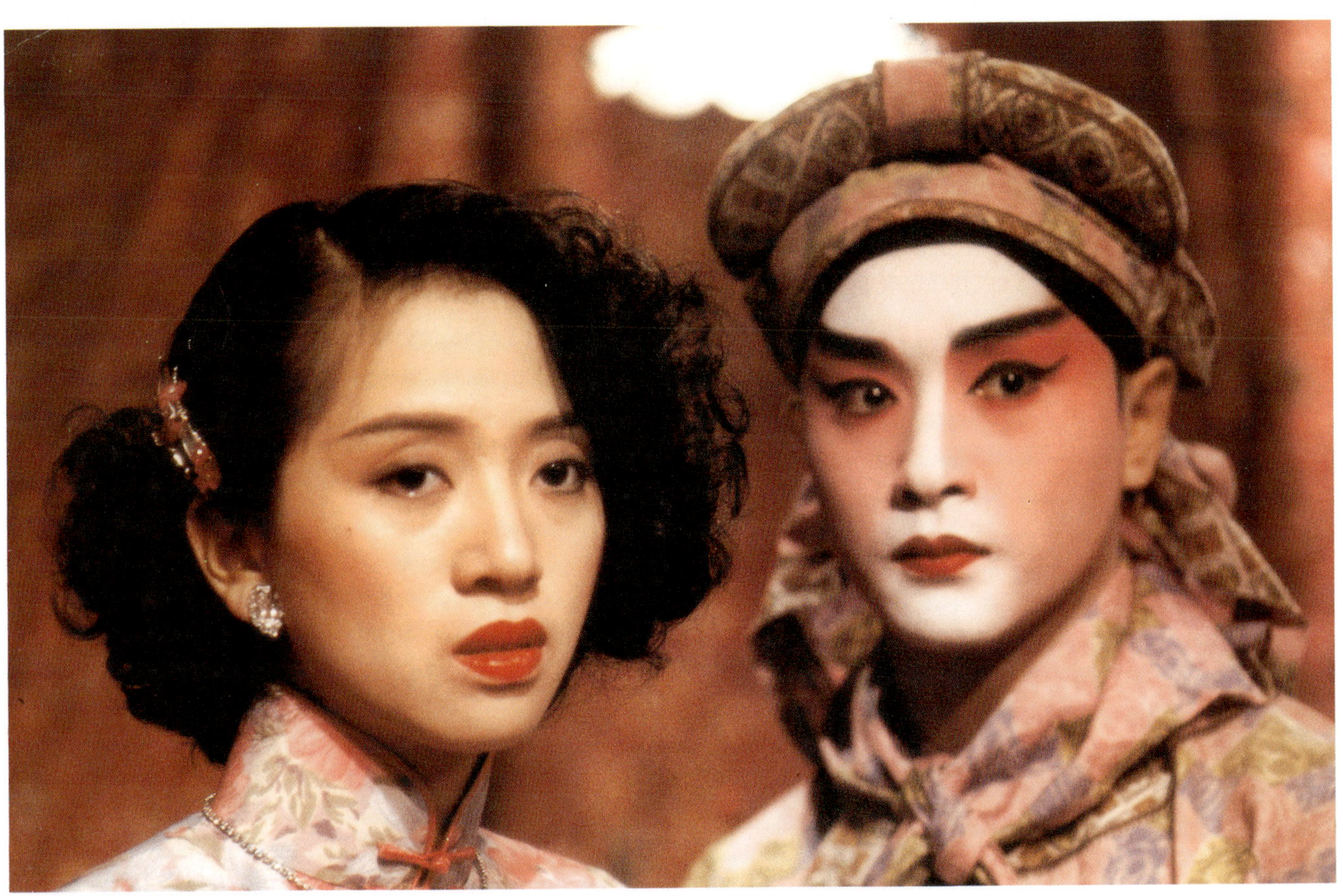

or their love. They choose to commit double suicide by eating the opium they had been so luxuriantly smoking during their relationship.

Now Fleur returns to 1987 to find her long-lost lover. As she says to the clerk, "Twelfth Master and I, we took opium to kill ourselves—by dying together we would be together forever. But when I went down, I couldn't find him. I couldn't bear it any longer, so I decided to come back to search for him."

The inspiration for this tale of double suicide can be traced to Stanley Kwan's childhood fascination with Cantonese opera. At age five he learned to sing and perform the lovers' final duet in *Di Nu Hua* (The Patriotic Princess, or Princess Cheong Peng). In this opera, the Ming dynasty falls. The princess escapes the rebel invasion of the palace, as well as her father's edict that all members of his family and court be put to death. Eventually she and her faithful suitor are to be married in the imperial court—under the new Qing emperor. But to escape the dishonor of submitting to another ruler, they decide to kill themselves. Alone in the garden, beneath the symbol of the entwining tree, they sing their sad and final duet:

> SHE: We had hoped to be happily married, but this was not to be. . . . In heaven or in hell, we shall never part. I wish to drink with you now.
>
> HE: Holding the cups and in tears, I put the poison in our wine.
>
> THEY: Let us drink our way onto the paths of eternity.

Clearly, this romantic love that ends in double suicide inspired Kwan, and he recreated the story in *Rouge,* weaving in both music and song. He updated the tale by adding both the modern couple as counterpoint and a twist in the plot: we discover that Twelfth Master escaped death to live on after Fleur. No longer are twentieth-century couples capable of sustaining such love as we find in the opera. But then, perhaps, they never were. Still, despite the dose of modern realism, our heart goes out to Fleur, whose undying romanticism brings her back from the land of shade, sixty years later, to search for her lost love.

ANN HUI: ACCIDENTAL SPECTATOR

The Spooky Bunch (1980), by Hong Kong director Ann Hui, is a delightful, rollicking comedy about an itinerant Cantonese opera troupe. The troupe has been hired for several days by a rich man, who is plotting to marry his grandson to the lead actress Ah Chi (Josephine Siao, also known as Siao Fong-fong) to get rid of a curse her grandfather cast on their family long ago. This troupe, like those in many theatrical companies the world over, is extremely superstitious. When moving into their hotel room, Ah Chi and her friend Maria hold a purification ceremony, sprinkling water about and chanting, "Excuse me, excuse me," presumably apologizing to those who may have previously occupied the premises. Before the first performance, the actors and crew light incense and bow before an altar set up behind the stage. (Today, a similar ritual takes place at the start of every Hong Kong film production.) But these efforts are in vain, because they have come to a place haunted by ghosts with scores to settle.

The Spooky Bunch came about when Siao approached Ann Hui and scriptwriter Joyce Chan to do a film about a Cantonese opera troupe, with a bit of ghost story tossed in. As background, Hui attended actual performances in the New Territories and on outlying islands, where the traveling troupes tour, and observed backstage life. Many of the actors for the film were recruited from a real Cantonese opera troupe led by a Mr. Leong, who ended up playing the troupe manager in the film, while his daughter played Ah Chi's rival. His son, Leong Siuhung, was a martial arts director for the movies. Thus the backstage story holds remarkable resonance for the film itself. There are additional opera connections in the film. The woman who plays Maria, Ah Chi's companion, is Zheng Mengxia, the wife of the famous Cantonese opera librettist Tang Disheng, who wrote *Di Nu Hua.* Tang Disheng wrote about forty librettos, and ten of them were extremely popular in the Cantonese opera repertoire. Zheng actually trained in opera under one of the most famous *dan* (one playing female roles) in Beijing, Xun Huisheng.

■ Director Ann Hui

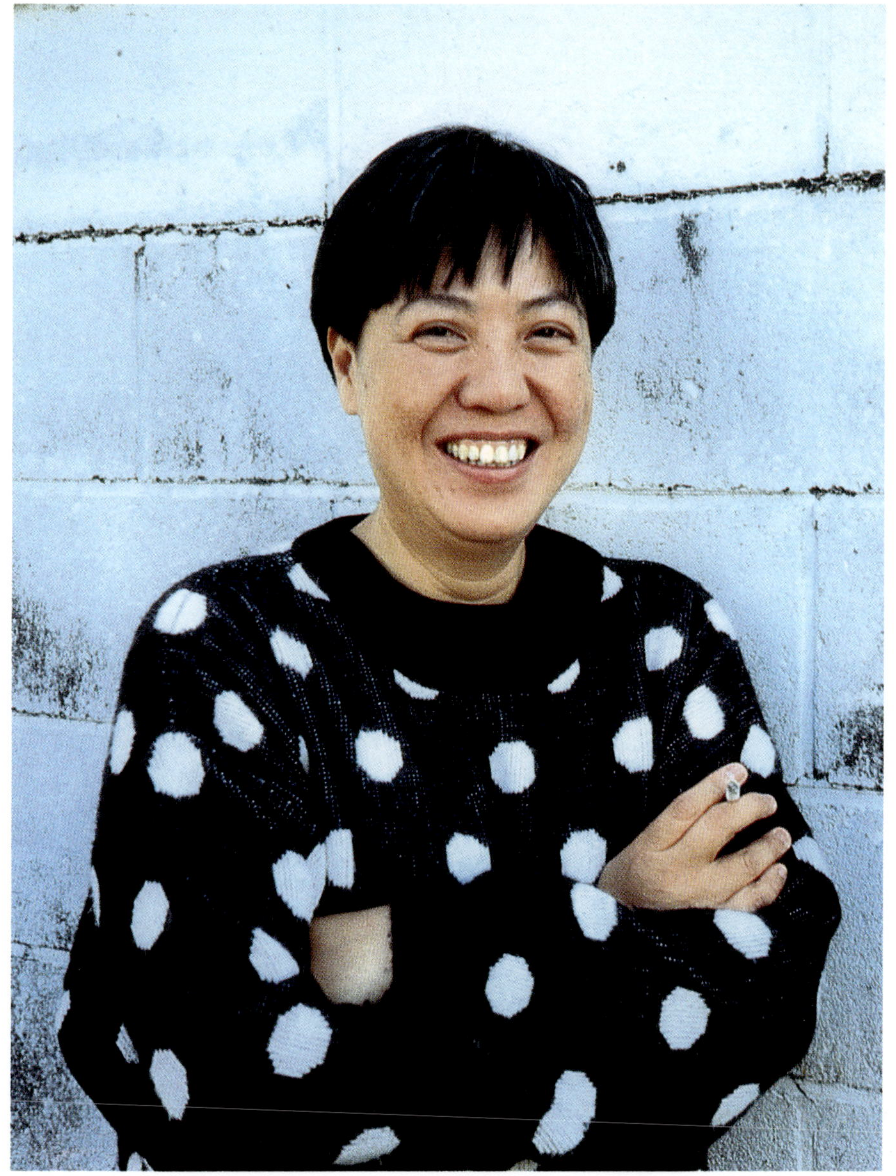

Although Ann Hui openly admits that opera does not interest her personally, she acknowledges her extensive exposure to Cantonese

■ Juxian, played by Gong Li, stars as Duan Xiaolou's (Zhang Fengyi) long-suffering wife in *Farewell My Concubine*.

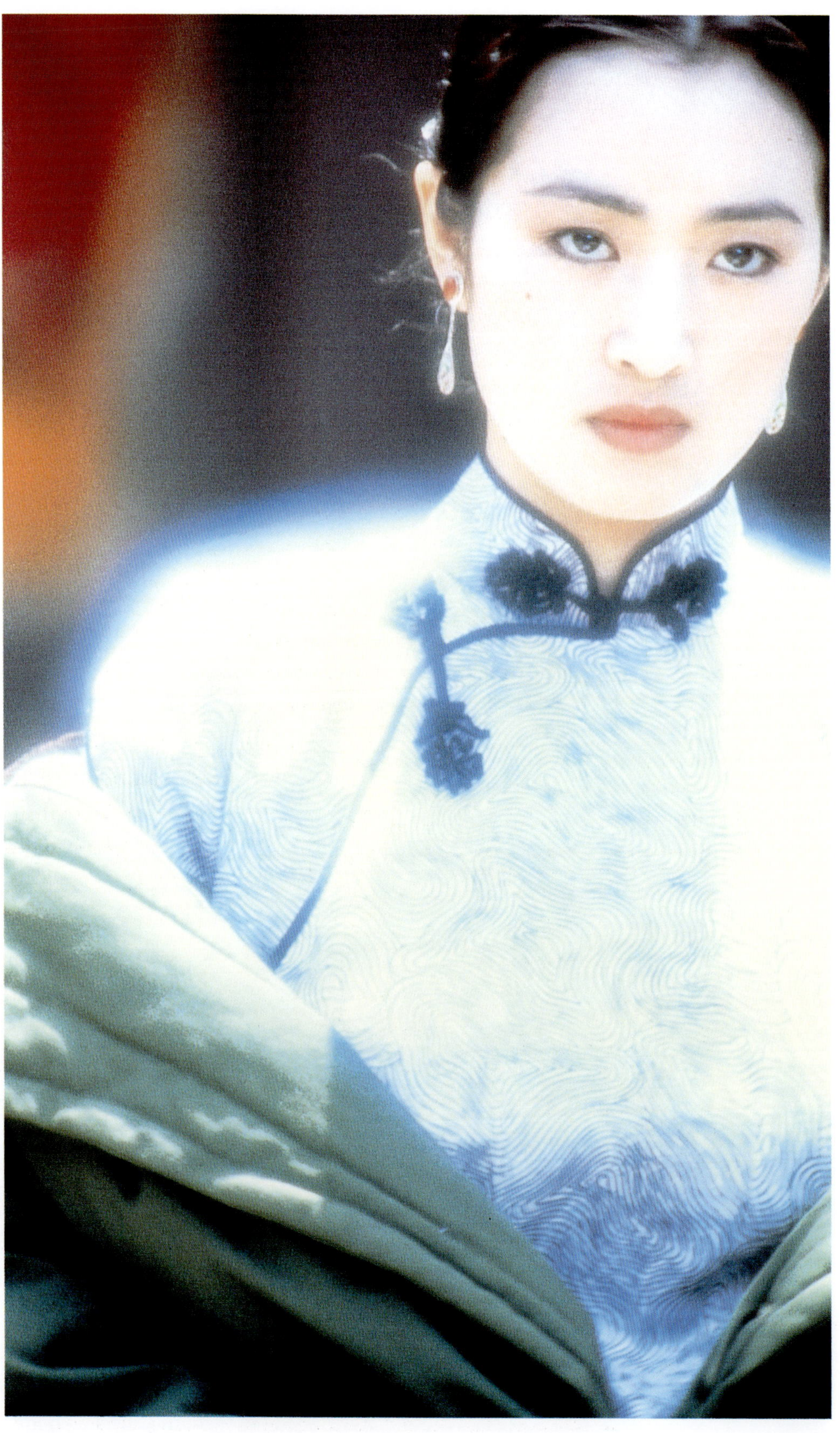

opera as a child. She was taken to live performances—at which the highlight for her was eating sweets and snacks—and she recalls often seeing movie renditions of Cantonese opera in the 1950s. She also acknowledges the influence of opera on filmmakers, especially those working on martial arts films. "If you ask these martial arts directors, at least half of them come from opera backgrounds," she says. "They derive a lot of their acrobatics from Beijing opera." She points out that "King Hu, who developed kung fu films, is actually a fan of Beijing opera." Hui has worked with King Hu, whose films *Come Drink with Me* (1966), *Dragon Gate Inn* (1967), and *A Touch of Zen* (1971) relaunched the martial arts genre.

Josephine Siao was one of the top actresses in Hong Kong in the 1960s, playing in teenage comedies and melodramas and also in early martial arts films. In her youth, she studied Cantonese opera quite seriously, as well as *bei pai* (Beijing opera fighting), for which her teacher was Fen Juhua, the famous opera master who also taught John Lone (*The Last Emperor,* 1987) and Hong Kong's top action director Ching Siutung.

Recently, Siao has returned to the silver screen, starring as the martial arts expert mother of martial arts whiz Jet Li in the two *Fang Shi Yu* movies. Learning from a real martial arts expert, she noted in a television interview that "this is the first time ever that I really know what martial arts is all about. Before it was more posing, and it was more Beijing opera stuff."

Tsui Hark, another one of Hong Kong's top action director-producers, has a deep interest in traditional Chinese arts. In his brilliant action comedy *Peking Opera Blues* (1986),[3] a film popular on the American art house and film festival circuit, he depicted the trials and tribulations of a Beijing opera troupe in Republican China, during a time of political turmoil. The twist is that the heroes of this film are heroines—three women whose fates collide—one of them played by superstar-actress Lin Chinghsia.

Interestingly enough, the Chinese title of the film is *Dao Ma Dan,* the term for a warrior woman in Chinese opera. (*Dao* means "sword," *ma* means "horse," and *dan* was the term for a female part in opera.) Another opera tradition is adopted, in an updated way, by having Lin appear first in male disguise: Chinese opera is replete with actors and actresses famous for playing roles of the opposite sex, including the legendary Mei Lanfang.

Even two years ago, as Lin prepared for another Tsui Hark production—a remake of King Hu's classic *Dragon Gate Inn*—she was asked to study some movements and postures from a Beijing opera actress. "Tsui Hark told me that *yen shen* [eye energy or power] would be very important to the movie," the actress says. It is key, as well, in Chinese opera. However, Lin adds, "The point is not to mimic what you learn from Beijing opera but to use your own method to express this movement, to capture the spirit of the movement, the stance."

CHEN KAIGE: GROWING UP IN OLD BEIJING

"The reason I love Beijing opera is because it really is the old-time Beijing," says Chen Kaige with a hint of nostalgia. His latest film, *Farewell My Concubine,* is about the friendship of two Beijing opera stars over fifty years of turbulent Chinese history. The story begins in the 1920s when Beijing opera was at the height of popularity. "If you belong to the human race, you go to the opera," as one opera master tells his students. "From the beginning of opera, it has never been so popular as it is today. You are lucky to be part of it."

Soft and effeminate Cheng Dieyi (Leslie Cheung) has been brought up since youth to play female roles opposite the reckless and charismatic Duan Xiaolou (Zhang Fengyi). Their most famous roles are the defeated emperor and his loyal concubine in the classic piece *Ba Wang Bie Ji* (The King Parts from His Concubine). (In fact, the Chinese title of the film is the title of opera.) Part of Cheng's success in his role is due to his personal identification with the concubine. As the theater manager says, "Has he not blurred the difference between theater and reality, between male and female?"

This blurring proves fatal, as Cheng harbors an unarticulated love for his co-star. Duan, on the other hand, clearly differentiates between stage and reality. He wants to lead his own offstage life, and he ends up marrying a headstrong courtesan (Gong Li), who becomes, in Cheng's mind, the "other woman." Meanwhile China falls to successive waves of conquerors, with the theater subject to the control and caprice of the Japanese in the 1930s, then the Guomindang, then the communists, then the vicious Red Guards of the Cultural Revolution.

The power and the beauty of Beijing opera are ravishingly captured in this film. Scenes from both practice and performance convey some of its hypnotic magic, as fantastically costumed bodies twirl across stage to the insistent beat of clappers and cymbals. In Duan's heroic emperor, we feel the grandeur of archetypes. "What kind of man was he," the schoolmaster lectures. "A peerless and invincible hero, but fate was not on his side." Cheng's self-sacrificing beauty is the female counterpart, who would rather die with her king than live on without him.

"Of course, Beijing opera is very important to this story," says Chen. "When I started to work on the film I spent a lot of time in the evenings looking at Beijing opera." He located two old opera theaters in Beijing, as well as one in Tianjin. Upon visiting these theaters, he says, "I heard the singing of Beijing opera. I heard a voice from my memory."

Chen believes that the story lines and the characterizations of Beijing opera "really reflect the [Chinese] way of thinking, according to Confucianism, that everything is so black and white. People are not used to thinking that human nature is a mixture. They want to know who is the villain, who is the good guy. People want to have the same thing in films." Perhaps that is why, he suggests, even the Hong Kong audience could not appreciate the complex role of Cheng Dieyi.[4]

Admittedly, opera as an art form is fading. "I'm not surprised Beijing opera is gone now because the old lifestyle [itself] is dead," Chen says. "In those days people enjoyed not being so busy." Then he adds with a smile, "I think opera will have a major revival fifty years from now."

CULTURAL CHANGE

Inevitably, the close ties between Chinese opera and film examined here will dissolve as younger generations drift away from Chinese opera and as film itself continues to create its own language. And why not? Chinese culture is changing. The ambiguities and vicissitudes of modern life cannot support the limited conventions that opera imposed on our consciousness. For me, the best of the new Chinese

■ Director Chen Kaige

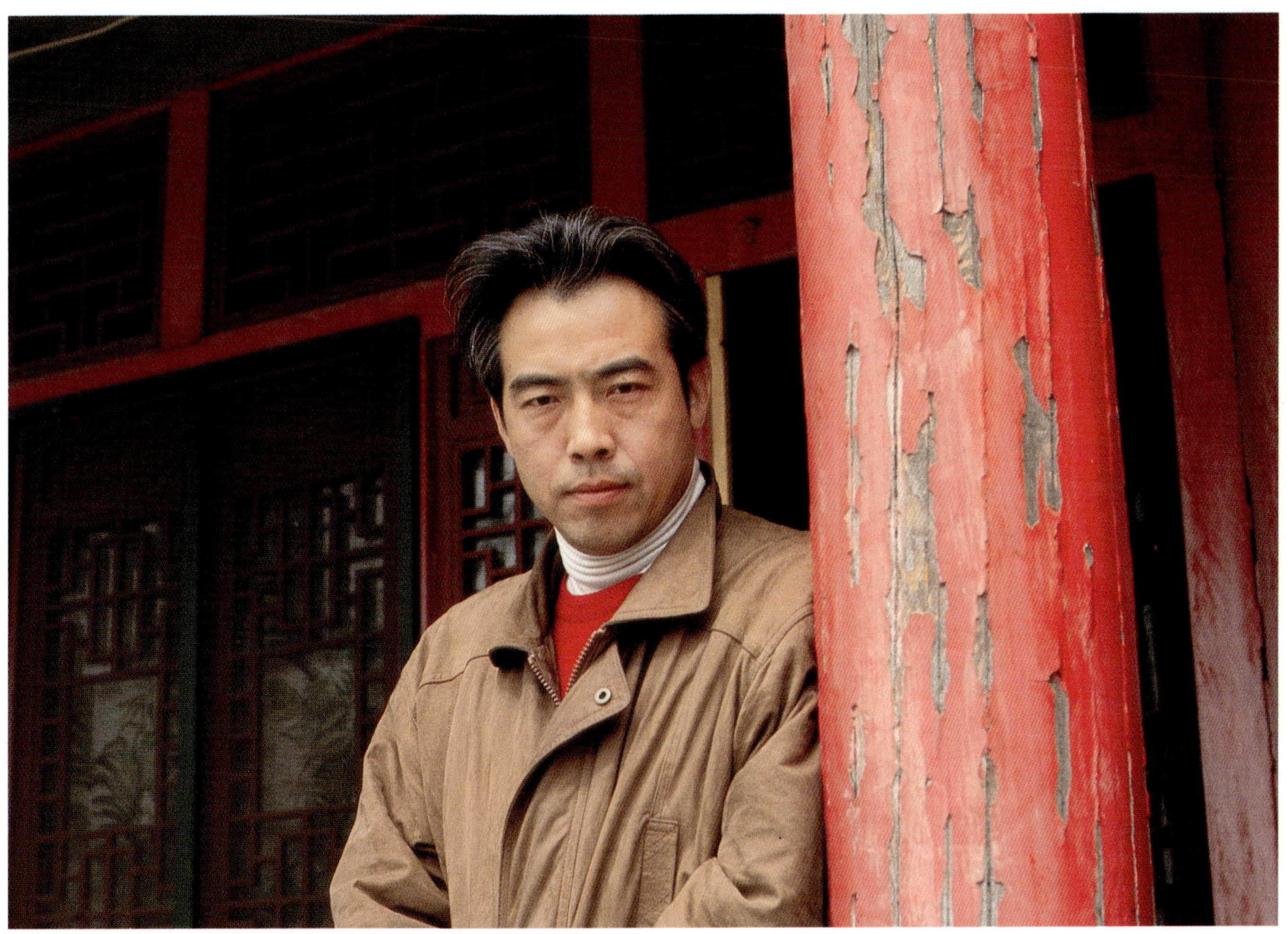

cinema—especially those works by the so-called Fifth Generation filmmakers—tries to take in some of the scope and ambiguity of human existence.

In the meantime, understanding the connections between the traditional art of opera and the young art of film is, I think, to understand something of the essence of being Chinese. ■

NOTES

Information and quotations in this essay are derived, in part, from the following interviews by the author: Shirley Chan, Hong Kong, July 15, 1993; Chen Kaige, Hong Kong, July 21, 1993; Stanley Kwan, Hong Kong, August 21, 1993; Lin Chinghsia, Hong Kong, August 22, 1993; Ann Hui, Hong Kong, September 12, 1993.

1. *Farewell My Concubine,* the film by Chen Kaige that won the Palme d'Or at the 1993 Cannes Film Festival, was released in the United States in the fall of that year. Most of the other films named in this essay are available on videotape at specialty video stores in major U.S. cities.

2. Catalogue for the 13th Hong Kong International Film Festival (Hong Kong: Urban Council, 1989), p. 94.

3. In the West, the northern style of Chinese opera is still often referred to as "Peking opera," since it has been known by that name for decades. However, since China's capital city is now commonly spelled as "Beijing" and the pinyin for this type of opera is *Beijing xi,* I have used the term "Beijing opera" throughout this essay except when "Peking opera" is in the given title of a film or book.

4. Another film that treats the confusion between life and stage is Huang Shuqin's *Woman Demon Human* (1987). In it a young girl growing up in a theatrical family is determined to become an opera actress, despite her father's wishes. First training with the troupe, she eventually goes away to the prestigious national opera school. Although she achieves great success, especially playing male roles, happiness in love eludes her. (There are no homosexual overtones, however, in this mainland-financed, mainland-produced film.) Finally she realizes, "I am married, married to the stage." Her dilemma is more happily resolved than the dilemma in *Farewell My Concubine.*

5. The so-called Fifth Generation was the first to be trained in filmmaking after the Cultural Revolution was over. Many of them, such as Chen Kaige, Li Shaohong (*Bloody Morning*), Tian Zhuangzhuang (*The Blue Kite*), and Zhang Yimou (*Raise the Red Lantern*), were graduates of the Beijing Film Academy.

■ Scarlet Cheng is the managing editor of *Asian Art News,* a Hong Kong magazine that focuses on the contemporary art and artists of Asia. She has written frequently on film and on the arts for such publications as the *Washington Post,* the *Asian Wall Street Journal,* and the *South China Morning Post.* In October 1993, she organized the "Fifth Generation of Chinese Filmmakers" festival for the Freer Gallery of Art, Smithsonian Institution, Washington, D.C. Born in Taiwan, Cheng grew up in the United States and now works in Hong Kong.

FURTHER READING

Berry, Chris, ed. *Perspectives on Chinese Cinema.* London: British Film Institute, 1991.

A collection of articles about the new Chinese cinema, very uneven in quality.

Li Cheuk-to et al. *Cantonese Opera Film.* Hong Kong: Urban Council/Eleventh Hong Kong International Film Festival, 1987.

A collection of essays about the period when Cantonese opera was one of the staples of Hong Kong film—the 1950s and early 1960s.

Teo, Stephen. "The Dao of King Hu." In *A Study of Hong Kong Cinema in the Seventies,* pp. 34–40. Hong Kong: Urban Council/Eighth Hong Kong International Film Festival, 1984.

An essay on the philosophies found in the films of King Hu (Hu Jinquan), whose martial art films of the latter 1960s and the 1970s defined the best of the genre during that period. These included *Come Drink with Me* (1966), *Dragon Gate Inn* (1967), and *A Touch of Zen* (1971).

Wu Zuguang, Huang Zuolin, and Mei Shaowu. *Peking Opera and Mei Lanfang.* Beijing: New World Press, 1981.

A charming little volume with a good overview of Beijing opera and translations from Mei Lanfang's autobiography.

SUBSCRIPTIONS

_____ I would like to begin my subscription to *Asian Art & Culture* starting with the current issue.

□ 1 year (3 issues): $37 □ 2 years (6 issues): $74 Institutional subscriptions:

□ outside U.S.: $49 □ outside U.S.: $98 □ 1 year (3 issues): $79 (outside U.S.: $91)

□ 2 years (6 issues): $158 (outside U.S.: $182)

AVAILABLE BACK ISSUES

Please send me the back issues marked below.

Total number of issues _____ x $15.95 each ($19.50 outside U.S.) = $ _____.

Institutions: For prices and discount information on back issues and complete back volumes, contact the Journals Department at Oxford University Press: 1-800-852-7323.

Coming in Fall 1994

HUMOR

The journal examines the lighter side of Asian culture in this look at humor in Chinese, Japanese, Islamic, and Indian art. Essays explore comic themes and traditions together with visual puns, satire, and amusing depictions of kings and characters in painting and literature. Contemporary artist Masami Teraoka discusses humor and social consciousness in his complex ukiyoe-style painting.

Smithsonian Associates receive a 20 percent discount on subscriptions and back-issue sales.

_____Vol. II, No. 1 Winter 1989
A Lyric Impulse in Japan

_____Vol. II, No. 2 Spring 1989
Timur and Fifteenth-Century Iran

_____Vol. II, No. 3 Summer 1989
Buddhist Art of South Asia

_____Vol. II, No. 4 Fall 1989
Raghubir Singh's Photographs of the Ganges, Mughal Gardens

_____Vol. III, No. 1 Winter 1990
Japanese Ceramics, Crafts

_____Vol. III, No. 2 Spring 1990
Ancient Chinese Music and Bronzes; Contemporary Chinese Folk Art

_____Vol. III, No. 3 Summer 1990
Yokohama Prints

_____Vol. III, No. 4 Fall 1990
The Dream Journey in China

_____Vol. IV, No. 1 Winter 1991
Games

_____Vol. IV, No. 2 Spring 1991
Indonesian Performing Arts

_____Vol. IV, No. 3 Summer 1991
East Asian Furniture

_____Vol. IV, No. 4 Fall 1991
Art Collecting

_____Vol. V, No. 1 Winter 1992
Ancient Mesopotamian Art in the Louvre

_____Vol. V, No. 2 Spring 1992
The Sense of Place in Japan

_____Vol. V, No. 3 Summer 1992
Indian Craft and Ritual

_____Vol. V, No. 4 Fall 1992
The Art of the Map

_____Vol. VI, No. 2 Spring 1993
Patronage by Women in Islamic Art

_____Vol. VI, No. 3 Summer 1993
Art and Architecture of Sri Lanka

_____Vol. VI, No. 4 Fall 1993
Indian Jewelry and Glass

_____Vol. VII, No. 1 Winter 1994
Vietnam

Send orders with payment and address changes to the Journals Department, Oxford University Press, 2001 Evans Road, Cary, N.C. 27513. Order by mail; by fax: (919) 677-1714; or by telephone: 1-800-852-7323. Individual subscriptions must be paid by personal check or credit card. All orders are shipped via surface mail. For air-expedited delivery to countries outside the U.S., add $5 (subscription and back issue orders).

_____ I enclose my check made payable to Oxford University Press.

_____ Please charge to my _____ MasterCard _____VISA _____American Express

Account number _____ Expiration date _____

Signature _____ *(Credit card order not valid without signature.)*

Name _____

Address _____

City/State/Zip _____ BC94BI

Smithsonian Associate membership number _____